A PORTRAIT OF ALL THE RUSSIAS

A PORTRAIT
OF ALL THE RUSSIAS

Laurens van der Post

Photographs by Burt Glinn

William Morrow & Company, Inc., New York 1967

The author and the photographer wish to express their gratiude to Mr. Harry Sions, and to Mr. Frank Zachary, Mr. Lou Mercier, and the late Mr. Ted Patrick of *Holiday* magazine for commissioning them for the original assignment out of which the present work has been developed.

Printed in Holland.

To Margaret Glinn
and Ingaret Giffard

Contents

I

Moscow

I must begin with the mood in which I took the journey to Russia if that journey is properly to be understood. For years I had been troubled by the image of Russia presented to us in the outside world. My own life has compelled me to travel much, and the process has convinced me that one never really knows another country unless one knows it through the life of the individuals who compose it. But my trouble with the Russian image was precisely that I could not discover a Russian individual in it. No matter what and how much I read or how closely I scrutinized my newspapers, the Russians remained a vast, uniform, impersonal, undifferentiated and forbiddingly ideological mass.

I felt this impediment keenly and even thought it dangerous. Nonetheless, my belief persisted that behind the opaque official front there was a man and his humanity to be discovered and honored, and that until this were done no real understanding between ourselves and the Russians would be possible. Whether I was overnaïve in thinking I could do this under the circumstances existing in the Soviet Union today, the account of my journey will show.

I set off on a lovely morning in April. At London Airport it struck me suddenly that the Soviet jet in which I was to fly to Moscow was keeping its crew very much to itself. The aircraft itself took some finding. It was tucked away on its own at the far corner, out of reach of casual contact with the English world around it. But I liked the look of its clean lines — it was painted cream with a little red, notably in the Soviet gift to the heraldry of our day, the hammer and sickle — and I found myself giving it an immediate vote of confidence. Then, in what seemed to me a remarkably short time, we were taxiing into take-off position on the runway. It was one of the most purposeful and streamlined departures I had ever experienced.

Presently a huge noonday meal arrived, unannounced by menu, wine list or inquiry of any kind — and with it came an unexpected demonstration of Russian gaiety. Having already eaten more than usual, I bowed myself out of the race over a cup of coffee. By way of apologizing to the grave young woman who was serving me the desserts, I pointed at a strained button. Instantly she laughed with pleasure, and the sudden change from a formal, almost melancholy expression into laughter was enchanting.

I felt utterly reproved for having suspected her of being incapable of fun, and I stress it here because it was my first encounter with what I believe is one of the most typical characteristics of the Russians. They are not a smiling people. With them the smile is generally only a preliminary to laughter, and this perhaps more than anything else gives them their reputation for melancholy. But for laughter itself the Russians have a great capacity and respect, and because this young air hostess was the first to show me the laugh behind the mask, I remember her with gratitude.

Meanwhile, it was amazing how on such a clear day the character of each country on the way to Moscow stood out on the ground below, even at 30,000 feet and at 600 miles per hour. After England, it was astonishing how often the Dutch scene looked managed, arranged in precise geometric patterns wherever river and ocean permitted. Germany was only a glimmer of yellow sand on the horizon, but Denmark was laid out neatly, polished like a soldier's equipment for inspection. The pattern appeared dedicated to a conception wherein everything, even beauty, was put to definite use.

Over Copenhagen the day was blurred with afternoon smoke, and I was dismayed by the speed with which our own pace, together with the sun's, had advanced the approach of night. The Baltic in that ash-blond light was a shallow shadow, and only after Riga, the capital of Latvia, did one see again a pattern of manufactured land. The change was startling, for the basic design of Europe was now asserted only by outposts, and these were threatened by an immense mass of featureless earth and forest advancing from the east. One was abandoned utterly to a level-topped vision of a strange flat earth stretching from horizon to horizon, its cover of forest rarely broken by any clearing or act of man, though it often gleamed with the burned-out silver of lakes, streams and marshes.

We landed at the international airport at Sheremetevo, less than twenty miles from Moscow, just before sundown. The air was surprisingly warm, the light like olive oil laying a gloss on the slender pines and birches of the woods that still crowd in on the Russian capital. The calm was immense, and not a shiver of air stirred the frail branches. Beyond the trees rose neither mountains, hills, mounds nor even towers. On such level earth, in so level an evening, the sky achieved its fullness on space and height, and that was something very Russian. Great as the effect of this immense land is on the senses, that of the sky is always greater.

After the bustle and noise of London Airport, the stillness here was astounding. While I was in the modest and unpretentious reception building, not a single aircraft arrived or left. It felt oddly isolated and provincial, as if I had arrived not at an entrance to one of the world's great capitals but in some remote country backwater.

Our reception in the airport building added to this impression. Gone was the formality which had seen us into the plane. Instead, a rural casualness characterized the persons who met us. I detected no sign of rigidity, arrogance or suspiciousness in my own reception. It is true there were still no smiles, but the customs and immigration officials stamped my declaration forms without reading them and passed my bag without opening it. All the time a young Intourist girl stood by me, telling me in admirable English what to do, and when it was done she summoned a car with a mere wave of the hand, so that in a remarkably short time I was on my way through the woods to Moscow.

Moscow stands at the center of the great Russian plain, but just beyond the woods some wind of time has raised a gentle ground swell in the earth. Breasting the first slow wave of land, I saw the city itself in the last light of the sun. I do not know precisely what I had expected but I was disappointed. From that distance I saw only putty-colored bricks and concrete slabs piled upon one another in huge square building blocks, like cakes of yellow soap heaped into unoriginal shapes. The closer we came to the city, the smaller appeared the power of invention in the vast design, and the few skyscrapers struck me as early Manhattan rather than Soviet in their inspiration.

What did impress me was the scale and a certain dynamic implicit in the scene. It was awe-inspiring to see this city of more than 7,000,000 people topping the slight swell of earth grandiosely spoken of as the Lenin Hills, and advancing over the passive plain to sweep wooden villages out of its way and take light concrete leaps over rivers, canals and streams. It was an advance as disciplined as that of a crack regiment. In that sense alone the scene contained some sort of counter to any feelings of disappointment aroused by the monotony and poverty of design.

The driver of my car certainly shared none of my misgivings. He was downright proud of it all. Speaking good German, he would point out some fresh, developing prospect and say, "There was a village there a year ago, and look at it now!" Once he indicated a gray apartment-house eminence and remarked, "I went by here yesterday and since then they have added three stories to it." He paused before adding proudly, "We have increased our capacity for prefabricated building so much that we now build faster than the Americans."

Now, for all I had seen up to this moment, Moscow might have been set down in a desert of history without a past of its own and only this stiff prefabricated present straining to repeat itself in the future. But suddenly, beyond the river filled to the brim with sunset colors, there was a flicker of fire and shape of flame. It came from the red-brick walls, turrets, spires and domes of the delicate sixteenth century Novo-Devichy Convent, a survivor of one of the earlier religious establishments which once earned Moscow the description of "City of Forty Times Forty Churches". The convent blossomed like a rose among the concrete cubes. It was as if I were witnessing in it a quiet assertion of faith in what is gentle, patient and mature in man — all very different from the furious all-out investment in the directed world which surrounded it.

We traveled on at an easy pace through the oddly silent and ordered streets between the tall buildings which line the new suburbs of Moscow. Although it was obviously one of the busiest hours of the day, the unusually wide, straight thoroughfares seemed curiously empty. Cars, buses, trucks, all of a strikingly uniform design, flowed easily in two broad streams. The pavements, too, were wide and the people on them seemed to be plodding doggedly in colorless masses between their huge impersonal apartment blocks. Their pace struck me as that of a country people trudging home from their fields, not the brisk step of persons leaving metropolitan offices.

That was one curious aspect of the first impression Moscow made on me. I had little feeling of being in a world capital. There was no impression of self-sufficiency, such as is instantly evoked in the visitor by London, Paris and Rome. On the contrary, my feeling was that of being somewhere deep in the country, in a huge village that had suddenly grossly exceeded itself. And I tended to go on feeling this everywhere in the city, except in the squares and streets around the Kremlin, where the glow of history became a leaping, vivid discovery. This odd complex of buildings, boxed in and overtopped by a vast new world of uniform structures, was enough to give Moscow the heart without which a city, no matter what its size, can never be great, and to make it a capital not just in the administrative and political sense but also in the imaginations and emotions of men.

It was already nearly dark, and I had barely had a glimpse of the Kremlin's towers and spires in the last iridescence of the day when we drew up outside my hotel, on the opposite side of the square facing them. The hotel was the National, built at the beginning of this century and looking even older from the outside. A doorman in a splendid Metro-Goldwyn-Mayer uniform came out to help me. To my surprise we ignored the reception desk and entered a long room labeled Service Bureau, the office maintained by Intourist in this as in all other hotels to which foreign tourists are sent.

The staff was entirely feminine, but younger and smarter in appearance than other women I had seen so far. Each girl sat at a desk and telephone of her own, gravely and self-assuredly doing what she could and had to do.

And that, I must confess in fairness to the travelers there, took a very long time: the National is a smallish hotel, yet it took the grave young lady dealing with me three quarters of an hour to discover the number of my room. She must have dialed thirty numbers in that time and rung off after a brief conversation, to begin all over again without trace of impatience or despair. In the end she handed me the number without apology or comment — or, of course, a smile.

My room on the third floor was vast. The ceiling seemed thrice as high as that of any hotel room I had ever known. I thought of course this was a peculiarity of the age to which the hotel belonged, but I was to find that this love of height is still deep in the Russian builder not only of skyscrapers and apartment houses but of coaches and trams as well. He will accept the need to economize on floor space and crowd his accommodation on the ground, but he insists on a sense of the sky for a ceiling, with the result that I have been in Russian apartments almost higher than they are either broad or long. As noticeable as was the size of my room so too was its old-fashioned atmosphere. There were curtains of Victorian lace on the high, wide windows and massive drapes of plush beside them. One thing that was modern was the telephone on my desk, only a telephone directory was missing.

I was up early on another lovely spring morning. Already a long queue was forming on the far side of the square for admission to Lenin's tomb. I had not long joined the tail end of the queue when the man in front of me turned around and asked, "Tourist?" I said yes, and at once he stepped aside and beckoned me forward. I hung back but he insisted, and from there on I was passed quickly forward. Whenever I hesitated, people around me combined to urge me on in the friendliest possible manner. It appeared a natural point of honor for them to yield their places to the foreigner in their midst.

In the process I had a striking glimpse of the astonishing variety of races who make up the Soviet Union. Ninety per cent of the people, I suspect, were visitors to Moscow. I did not know Russia or the Soviet Union well enough to tell Russians, Byelo-Russians, Ukrainians, Lithuanians and Moldavians apart. All I could do was to see them as an interrelated group, clearly distinguishable from the others. More than half this group seemed to belong to the same indeterminate types as the rest of us Europeans. With different clothes and haircuts, physically they could have been British, French or Scandinavian.

How different, however, the impression of the non-Europeans in the queue! Georgians, Armenians, Uzbeks, Tartars, Turkomans, Azerbaijanians, Mongols and Buryats, to name only a few of the minority races the Soviet have forcibly bound in their iron union, stood out distinctively from the Europeans by their build, mold of face, cast of eye and texture. About none of these was there any of the feeling of boundless impersonal nature

Page 17 The May Day parade in Red Square, presided over by the towers of St. Basil's; 18-19 Family picnic on a Sunday in Sokolniki park; 20 Three women wait to buy holy water in the monastery grounds in Zagorsk; 21 Children in costume for a play at Peredelkino, the writers colony outside Moscow; 22-23 Soldiers on leave in Red Square, the country's first tourist attraction; 24 A blacksmith in his shop in Bukhara; 25 Oistrakh, the great violinist, listens to a student's exercises; 26 A resident of Baikal shows the Mongolian strain in the Siberian population; 27 Nadyezda Zaglada, the heroine of Soviet labor, a Ukrainian farm woman whose appearance at important events and congresses is constant; 28-29 Russian cow herders in the Steppe country; 30 Three Jews in the only remaining synagogue in Bukhara, formerly the most important Jewish center of Central Asia; 31 A merchant in the marketplace at Tashkent; 32 The long line waiting to enter Lenin's tomb waits patiently winter and summer, through heat and cold.

that the Slavs gave out. An outward-bound temperament, vivid and individual, was near the surface of their spirit, glowing in the eye and imparting if not always *élan* and pride then at least a certain separateness to their personality.

When at last I turned the corner into Red Square, Lenin's tomb added to the growing sense of paradox in me. At first glance it seemed as complete and arbitrary a break with the past as the Russian Revolution seems to those with only a surface knowledge of Russian character. Made mainly of red granite so deep in color as to be almost black, it might have been designed by an inferior and fanatical convert to Cubism in the earlier days. There was not a curve in its lines. Its shape was so uncompromisingly rectangular that it seemed to have bypassed both heart and imagination. It drove a chill through me as an act of the will committed without reference to its human context to the execution of one single idea.

I passed between two young sentries with pale blue eyes and earnest, open faces — and the best-polished boots I was ever to see in the Soviet Union. I went down the stairs under a yellow artificial light. For the first time I sniffed the smell of a Russian crowd, which I was to encounter in all public places, waiting rooms, planes, buses and trains in the Soviet Union, a whiff of a laundry basket on the weekly collection morning.

I turned right into a square inner chamber and there lay Lenin, Russia's one and only mummy. In the neon light he looked extraordinarily like a wax model of himself in Madame Tussaud's in London. His sandy-colored beard was trim and pointed, and everything about him was neat. He looked like what his disciples most abhor: a typical early twentieth century *petit bourgeois*. That this perishable being should have been enshrined as an imperishable image struck me as profoundly significant. Officially Russia may have abolished God, yet other gods have moved in to occupy the vacant spaces left in the Soviet spirit. And the god of gods lay there before me. I was in the tomb only a few minutes, yet I came out into daylight feeling as if I had just emerged from a pit of time.

My plane for Central Asia, where I had decided to begin my real journey, was due to leave at midnight. I had ample time, my guide informed me, to spend the evening at the ballet, theater, opera or circus. I rejected the first three because I thought a circus might bring me nearer to the ordinary people of Russia. Besides, I have loved circuses since childhood and had not seen one for many years. I never regretted the choice. I enjoyed myself so much that night at the Moscow Circus, and learned so much from it, that wherever I went in the months to come I never missed a circus.

The circus has a permanent home in all the major cities of the Soviet Union, and in the blueprints of the new towns springing up all over the country, a circus building is included side by side with the schools, sanatoria, palaces of culture, theaters, concert halls and other places of entertainment. The circus at the great industrial town of Rostov-on-Don, with its front of soaring Corinthian columns and classical gables, all patiently reconstructed after the destruction of the town by Hitler's hordes, looked like a Ruritanian opera house. Inside, it has more glittering tiers than a Hollywood wedding cake.

Over and over again, in Russian circuses, I was to feel that I was witnessing the continuation of a tradition founded by gladiators and tempered in the hungry arenas and implacable amphitheaters of Rome and Byzantium. The response of the toil-worn crowds in their shabby clothes added to that impression. Sealed off for generations from the outside world, as was the ancient world by its ignorance, they would look, their faces naked with wonder, at the appearance in the ring of the lions, apes, leopards, hippopotamuses and pythons, until a living bond was forged between spectators and performers.

At Rostov I saw a beautiful young Armenian girl, after taking what seemed to me far more than legitimate risks on a trapeze, so fired by the response of the crowd that she went further still. Her attendants produced an enormous black eagle, dark as one of Macbeth's midnight hags. This giant bird was unhooded and placed on the upper bar of the trapeze without being tied or secured to it in any way. It perched there swaying, balancing itself with its wings outstretched, its eyes green and hard with angry apprehension above a beak sharp as a Saracen's scimitar. Its talons were so long that they seemed to go twice around the bar of the trapeze and were strong enough to have carried off many a lamb to some clifftop.

Now this slender young girl seized the lower bar of the trapeze in one hand and had herself hoisted about a hundred feet above the ring. There she began to swing high and fast from one side of the dome to the other. By this time all lights were out except a solitary spotlight trained on the eagle and the girl as they swung violently through what now looked like empty and unsupported space. The eagle's wings stretched wider, trembling. It looked as if at any moment it might fly off and attack the slight, sequined figure of the girl. From time to time, in fact, the two of them swung so fast it seemed the eagle had her in its talons and was carrying her off into the night.

At the climax she went through a terrifying series of turns and aerobatics on the trapeze, until finally she was left hanging by one foot, zooming like a swallow through space with her arms stretched out and smiling with a strange ecstatic expression on her young face. Meanwhile the eagle looked down on her, growing ever blacker, angrier and more frenzied, as if he were the earthbound one and she had the wings. There before our eyes, so high above the sawdust of the ring, without a net spread out below to break the impact should she fall, her act turned into a strange, compelling kind of heraldry.

The acts done with wild animals and horses were equally astonishing. Here there was an identification of man and animal and a communication which I think we have lost in the West. With the horses in particular, the skill and color of Tatary and the Golden Horde were added to those on Byzantium and Rome. There was nothing, it seemed, man could not do with a horse. In addition to much wild and daring riding, I saw troops of Cossack and Armenian horsemen attack one another with glittering foils and a savage skill and abandon that seemed only a saber edge away from the real thing.

As for the wild animals, no two acts were ever alike. The tigers especially were superb. At Alma-Ata I saw the finest assembly of Siberian tigers looking as if they had stepped straight out of Blake's poem to burn bright in some forest of the night. I also made friends with the man who tamed them.

It all began in a curious way. I had wakened one night, startled, thinking I had heard a lion purring in my room. I had switched on the light and come to the conclusion that, out of homesickness for my native Africa, I had dreamed the sound. Coming back to my hotel for lunch the next day, however, I discovered the real explanation. A dense crowd had gathered in front of the hotel and everyone was looking up at a window next to my own on the second floor. There a huge tiger was looking down benignly at the crowd, and sitting on its back was a little girl with yellow curls. Beside the tiger stood the child's attractive young mother and her father, a tall man with deep-blue eyes and a sad face.

From the man I learned a great deal about circuses, and what he told me brought home the profound love the ordinary Russian has of the natural things of his native country. He himself had started life as a trainer of dogs. When I asked why he no longer trained them he said, "Because of the war." Apparently when Hitler's armies seemed invincible, he had been made to train dogs to dash out snapping at the heels of tanks. Then he would take them into the battle areas, strap contact mines on their backs and set them at armored vehicles.

"It was better than sacrificing our own men, of course," he explained; "but to me it was treachery, and ever since then I have felt that I lost the right to train dogs."

Often workers from a single factory will buy up all the tickets for a circus performance and pour into it together. The feeling of *being together* which they communicate on these occasions has an extraordinary, almost tangible power. Whatever else happens to most Russians in life, it is this emotion, I believe, which they prize above all others. Bored with his palaces of culture, denied access to the best ballet, opera and theater by a subtle system of privilege that the new technological, artistic and power aristocracy in Russia has created for itself, the ordinary citizen comes to his circus as much to overcome a growing sense of separation as to be entertained.

I managed to step into just such an audience once in Rostov, where the workers of a leather factory had taken over the entire circus. As the evening went by, this feeling of solidarity became so marked that I felt in danger of losing my identity. There were moments when I ceased to feel a foreigner — and for all the friendliness I encountered in the Soviet Union, I felt more of a foreigner there than in any country I have ever been in, even Japan.

In between the acts the workers proudly promenaded up and down the marble corridors of the building. On all floors, in the shining entrance halls with their granite floors and Greek pillars as well as in the restaurants and cafeterias, the factory hands played dance music. Everybody danced with everybody else, and I myself saw nothing strange in waltzing around the floor with an unknown young woman who came up and asked me to dance. The sense of togetherness had gone far beyond words, and only the dance, in its unity of movement in music and body and sexes, could express it.

The evening was, I am certain, significantly Russian, woven of the authentic stuff of the national spirit. And because something of all this was implicit in my experience at my first circus that night in Moscow, I have felt compelled to deal with it here near the beginning.

Another thing that emerged most clearly at Moscow was the contemporary aspect of the circus. There were, for example, all sorts of skits satirizing bureaucracy. This was not surprising because the campaign against the bureaucrat and red tape has the official sanction of the Party and is all the rage in the Soviet Union. Newspapers, comedians, clowns, private citizens can all rail as much as they like against bureaucracy, provided they do not blame the Party or its leaders for it.

After the performance I walked back to my hotel. Early as it was, the streets were nearly empty. The windows of the buildings were already dark. People in Russia, even in the capital, go to bed early. There are no night clubs, no prostitutes walking the streets and almost no policemen or "militiamen," as the Russians call them. I saw instead a patrol of young people of both sexes, with red bands around their arms, who everywhere volunteer for the duty of keeping public order. They went by looking bored and unemployed. I was not surprised, for no capital could have looked more law-abiding than Moscow did just then, as if it were inhabited not by men and women of the world but by the villagers that I suspect most Russians still are in their secret hearts.

II

Central Asia and the Caspian

It was another story at Vnukovo Airport, whence I was to fly to Tashkent. Even at midnight the place was as active as Etna in full eruption. The noise of aircraft arriving and taking off was incessant. The brilliantly lit departure halls and restaurants were crowded. On benches, against the walls and in the corners sprawled weary travelers, propped against their bundles and waiting with silent, uncomplaining patience for a seat to turn up in the crowded planes. During all the time I was in the Soviet Union I only once traveled in a plane with a seat to spare.

Here again, as at Lenin's tomb, I was moved to the front so that I could have first choice of the unoccupied seats. Again I had to make my peace with the sight of scores of tired people being turned back at the barriers, but there was something frightening, too, about the silent acceptance of fate implicit in their expressions and attitudes. In that moment I became aware of another characteristic of the Russian people which had been nagging at my mind for recognition ever since my arrival and which subsequent experience confirmed. They have an overwhelming instinct to conform, a tendency to be incapable of doing openly what others are not doing, or of challenging authority on a specific issue.

At my table in the aircraft were an Armenian colonel in the Soviet army and two Russian civilians. Presently the lateness of the hour overcame the colonel and one of the civilians and they fell asleep. I, however, could not

40

sleep. At one point I looked up and found the Russian who was still awake watching me, as if wanting to talk. I had been looking out of my window down at the earth and had felt amazed how, even in the dark, the sheer size of the country got through to one. I mentioned this to my companion. He warmed to my remark at once and began talking about the land of the Soviet Union. He talked unusually well. Russians, I found, were at their best when traveling. Physically and mentally they are people still on a journey, and so journeys release them from complex reserves and fears of all kinds and set them talking naturally and openly. He was no exception, and moreover he knew the Soviet Union well. He was, I discovered, a distinguished and widely traveled person.

It was right, he told me, to begin with a feeling of the immensity of the land. I must build on that as perhaps the greatest single fact necessary for understanding his people and his country. He wished he could convey all that immensity to me not just as a physical fact but also as the emotion that it was in him and all his countrymen. To begin with, did I realize that the Soviet Union was more than double the size of the continental United States? That it was almost three times the size of Australia, bigger than South America and only a third smaller than Africa?

In the west its territory began at the Polish frontier near Kaliningrad, in a long yellow spit of sand running out from the southern Baltic shore into a shallow gray sea, and stretched in one unbroken mass eastward for more than 6,000 miles to Cape Dezhnev on the Chukotski Peninsula. Indeed even that was not the end, for one would have to go out into the Bering Strait to Ratmanov Island to find there, on the frontiers of America's newest state, the easternmost extremity of Soviet territory.

"I have spoken there," he said, his pale gray eyes twinkling, "with Soviet and American Eskimos and could not tell the difference between them. Nor could they."

So wide apart are the two extremities of land that it is noon in one when it is not far from midnight in the other. The southernmost point of the Soviet Union was near Kushka on the borders of Afghanistan, perhaps 2,000 miles from the Equator. The northernmost point was well inside the Arctic Circle at Cape Chelyuskin in Siberia, a bare 800 miles from the Pole.

These two ends were more than 4,000 miles apart, and tremendous seasonal differences lay between them. In an hour or two, for instance, we would be flying over south Turkmenia, where spring comes in January. There the winter was short and could hardly be called winter at all. But in the north, at Cape Chelyuskin, even in midsummer the winds still piled up giant hummocks of ice on the shore. Already, in Turkmenia, plowing and sowing would be finished and spring nearly gone, but in Uzbekistan, where we would land in a few hours, we would find the earth aglow with purple heliotrope, scarlet poppies and wild red tulips. Yet the apple trees around Moscow would not blossom until late in May. In the far north of Siberia the tundra rivers would not be free of ice until the end of June, and by August the ice and frost would again start their southward march. In the extreme south the bamboo shot up at the rate of a yard a day. On the northern Siberian shore it took the straggling larches a century to grow to the thickness of a man's middle finger. In the south they would already be harvesting the grain while in Kamchatka the snow was still falling.

That, measured in the seasons, was the physical frame of the Soviet Union, but inside this had to be fitted the massive and endless diversity of detail. To start with there were the rivers. He started with them, he said, because he believed the history of Russians as a conscious and separate people began with the rivers. It was the rivers that first gave these people a meaning in the emerging world and a way of communicating with one another and with the civilizations and commerce of antiquity.

And surely no land on earth was ever blessed with such streams! Even to this day the length of navigable rivers in the Soviet Union exceeded the mileage of its extensive railway system. The great rivers flowed north, west, east and south. Some of the greatest never even reached the sea, so vast was the land: the Volga flowed 2,300 miles from its source in the middle of the Great Russian plain and finished in the land-locked Caspian in the far south; and the Amu Darya and Syr Darya, two of the greatest rivers of Central Asia, just fed the enclosed Aral Sea. Above all, he said, I must not forget the Siberian rivers, which were perhaps the greatest — such as the Yenisei, which was over 2,300 miles long. The rivers of European Russia flowed, he would say, out of history into the present. The rivers of Siberia and the Far East flowed out of the present into the future of his land.

Then there were the seas, inner and outer. Did I realize that the Soviet Union was a great sea power, that its coastline was twice the length of its land frontiers? Three of the world's oceans lapped at the Soviet earth in twelve seas, each one different. Thus the Black Sea did not freeze in winter, but up north the Kara Sea was dotted with ice floes even in summer. In the Baltic the difference between high and low tide is only a few inches, but in the Penzhina inlet of the Sea of Okhotsk it is thirty-four feet. As for the lakes, they varied from the world's largest, the Caspian, to the deepest, Lake Baikal.

There were also great mountain ranges, from the Pamirs rising fiercely to their crowning summit in the 24,590-foot Communism Peak to the ancient and gentle Urals, whose highest point, Narodnaya, attains a mere 6,184 feet. There were valleys where life had to breathe deep and fast to survive at an average level of more than three miles above the sea. And there was the descent of all this tossed and tormented earth into the great plains to the west and north of the Ukraine, plains where he had sat on his horse amid grass so high that the yellow tassels brushed his lips, the same plains which, when they were autumn-bare, were filled only with sky and space. He spoke of these plains with a warmth that not even the rivers had raised in him. Clearly the core of his spirit, like that of his people, was a wide, wide plain.

Then east of the plains, he continued, came the plateaus and hills of

Siberia, and then the earth became inflamed again until, in Kamchatka, it erupted in one of the world's highest volcanoes, that spitfire called Klyuchevskaya Sopka. But oh, the distances, he stressed, the worlds between its fires and the cold Pamirs, where the largest known glacier in the world, the Fedchenko, inched its way through time into the abysmal valleys below. In one world there were evergreen palms, the lotus flower of Egypt, roses, hump-backed oxen, camels and pink flamingos, while in the other were dwarf birches, violets amid snow drifts, wolves with Titian fur, and the Arctic owl. Then again, north of the plains and the fertile steppes were the forests, the greatest forest area on earth, so dense that at noon on a dull day he had to use a lamp to find his way through them. In the south, hard against the mountains, lay the extreme desert of sand burned bare by the sun; in the north lay the tundra, stripped naked by frost and long winds and white with the dust blown from the brittle ice which lies on the permanently frozen earth: two kinds of desert, each with its own challenge to the people of his land.

There were, too, the great, strange, forbidding islands. In the north, Franz Josef Land, Novaya Zemlya, the New Siberian Islands and Wrangel Island were all of frozen, inhospitable earth with black cliffs, white bergs and hardly a tree. But now, through permanent occupation and scientific research, they were found to have remarkable mineral riches. His people, he said, possessed a greater capacity for meeting the challenges of winter, solitude and physical hardship than any other.

From these islands, which with their new icebreakers they could keep open for three months a year, one could go down through the Bering Strait to the other islands, Ratmanov, the Commander Islands, the Kurils and Sakhalin. Here, thanks to a warm Pacific current and the volcanic earth, life was somewhat easier and more abundant. In the Kurils and Kamchatka alone there were dozens upon dozens of volcanoes, of which a great many were active. The bird and sea life there was incredible. White whales rolled, huffed and puffed in the waves, blowing fountains of pearl into the air.

He had even seen islands so packed with birds, seals and walruses that it was impossible to walk on their soil.

All this far-flung and diverse land had as its singular human contact some 220,000,000 people of 185 different ethnic and racial groups. These groups were organized into a hundred separate nationalities and concentrated in the fifteen republics that constitute the Soviet Union of today.

There then — he drew breath — were some of the relevant facts, but how convey the emotion? He would have to be a poet, painter, dancer and musician to do so. He could only suggest I listen to Russian music with an alert ear, for he believed that one characteristic which distinguished it from the music of other countries was that it had within it just such an immensity of scale. It expressed the great space and the vast silences. The song of the first bird at dawn, the vast stillness of the night, the howl of wolves on the rim of the Siberian plains; the sound of a hunter's horn in the vast forests of Russia, the wings of the wild swans beating the air over a Siberian river where ice is beginning to form along the banks, the wind stirring before the rain in high grass on the steppes, the voice of boatman calling to boatman — all these were sounds coming from afar and going farther still. Today there were other sounds and new rhythms to be added: the hum of hydroelectric turbines, factory sirens and the exhausts of tractors breaking the silences of woods and plains. But the bigness of the land was still under-·neath and dominant over all. In between one note and another the same great silence and space claimed everything. It might be melancholy, but it was a noble sadness.

Look at Russia's history, too. The dominant factor there was the greatness of their land. Invaded as no other country, perhaps, in the history of the world, with no initial barrier of sea or mountain to protect them, they survived because the bigness of the land defeated the invaders. Not only from external invaders, my friend added, but from all the tyrants and despots who made slaves of the people by invading from within. Always there was room for escape, even against native oppressors — places like the great forests of the north, the marshes of the Don — and increasingly Siberia, which ironically was both a region of exile and a home of freedom and independence for the Russian spirit.

Did the young people, I asked, feel about their history as he did? Even more strongly, he replied. They believed that the people and the land made Russia what it was, and would continue to make it what it would be in the future, whatever the appearances to the contrary might be.

At this point a sign flashed the word that we were about to land. I said good-by to my friend, and he thanked me for the chance I had given him of talking with a foreigner *dusha-dushi* — "soul to soul," a form of rapport I discovered was most important to Russians. I thought that was the last I would see of him, as I was leaving within the hour for Alma-Ata, but happily I was wrong.

I began my meeting with Central Asia in the dawn, high up in the air between Tashkent and Alma-Ata. Away to the southeast the sky was without cloud or haze, and flamingo-pink with cold. The earth was still in the dark, but the mountains of Kirghizia and Tadzhikistan were already visible, royal with height and solemn with snow, flying the colors of the dawn like battle flags from their crests. So impressive were they that it was difficult to realize that they were still only foothills in the greatest complex of mountains in the world, part of the same terrible vortex in the heart of the earth which reaches its climax in the Himalayas.

To the west and northwest, however, as the sun found the earth, the land fell away quickly into low hills and far away produced a shimmer and a blur which belonged to the dry, flat plain. This contrast reached its most dramatic expression at Alma-Ata, for there in front of us the T'ien Shans, or Mountains of Heaven, rose sheerly out of the lowland of Kazakhstan like a wall, with watchtowers 15,000 and 17,000 feet high under permanent snow. Behind us lay the diminishing valleys and the edge of the great brown plains where long patches of earth were under the plow. This immense theatrical backdrop of mountains on the orderly agricultural scene remains most vividly in my mind.

Between the airport and the city, the road was dense with traffic, most of it heavy trucks. I counted seventy trucks before I saw one private car.

"Why is the road so crowded?" I asked the young Russian who was my guide, seeing no destination for the traffic except the silent mountains.

"This is the main road to China. The frontier is only about one hundred and fifty miles away." But for all its nearness to China, the city of Alma-Ata in appearance was essentially Russian. As recently as 1933 its population was just over fifty thousand, almost all of it Russian. Then Stalin's planners and economists had taken it in hand. Today it is a city of half a million people, with two thirds of them still Russian.

This kind of expansion meant that inevitably, on the outskirts, there were those stiff regimental apartment blocks I had seen outside Moscow and was to see in every town and city from Central Asia to the suburbs of Leningrad and from Moscow to the Pacific Ocean. I asked to see one of these new apartments and was told it was impossible. The girl who was my guide at the time consoled me by saying, "You'll have plenty of time to see new apartments in other cities later on."

"But they will not be the same," I protested.

"Don't worry," she said gravely. "They are all the same wherever you go in the Soviet Union."

Taken aback, I exclaimed, "But don't you find it depressing to have the same apartments for everyone everywhere?"

She bristled at that and reproved me. "Why should I want anything different from what my fellow citizens have? What is good for one is good for all. We are all equal in the Soviet Union."

To me, this was one more elementary lesson, delivered there against that backdrop of mountains no two of which were alike. What we value as expressions of individual taste can easily be suspect in the Soviet Union as forms of dangerous self-indulgence, bourgeois deviationism and lack of solidarity.

In the days that followed, as I moved in and about the country around Alma-Ata, another and more positive impression grew in me. There was no mistaking a sense of purpose, of direction and of belief in the future. People were trying to build where there had been no building before. It was not building to my taste, but was it not better than no building at all? And ultimately did it not have a power of increase? The collective farms I saw may have been isolated show pieces, but they set an example where there had been none before. There was the shining proof of irrigation canals and conducted streams vanishing into the shimmer and dust of the hot, dry plains. I could understand the Russian pride in them all.

Below the line of beautiful T'ien Shan firs, the herdsmen were moving their great flocks from one sheltered slope and meadow to another. The whole country seemed on the move, cattle above and sheep below. On the plains the tractors threw up a chocolate dust behind their plows, and at noon the bare wooden State farm centers, austere and insufficient like encampments built in a military emergency, were almost empty because most of their people were out working the land.

Many a herdsman rode by with a karakul hat on his head. Deeper in the hills, some even wore the black and white felt hats and quilts of Kirghizia as they stood guard over their flocks. But most of them wore cloth caps and pale blue raincoats straight from the nearest clothing factory. The horses alone still evoked the memory of Genghis Khan. They had slim ankles, sturdy barrels, shaggy necks and proud heads that lifted easily. They might have been modeled on the horses dug out of some Manchu tomb. Their step was quick and electric and made an exciting sound on the earth as precise as any percussion instrument. Their riders rode them as if they had been

Page 49 The beautiful and ancient wall of the public square in Samarkand, the city of Tamerlane; 50 An old Uzbek sits outside the ancient city walls of Bukhara; 51 Turkoman shepherds in bivouac in the Kyzyl-Kum Desert; 52 Rug maker in Ashkhabad. The ancient designs of the Turkoman have given way to the recording of modern Soviet history as seen in the pattern on the wall; 53 Cotton farmer outside Tashkent; 54 The parking lot on market day in the village of Guzhdavan; 55 Women gossip in the marketplace of Guzhdavan; 56 A teahouse on the walls of a reservoir in Bukhara, dating from the days of Tamerlane.

born to them, reared on their milk and nourished on their blood, like the ancient Tatar hordes.

Among the mountains near Alma-Ata were skiing slopes, Olympic-size skating rinks, and above all an observatory manned by scientists as dedicated as any in the world. To me they appeared utterly detached from the growing city below them and completely interested in the beautiful nebula of Andromeda, which was their specialty. In the city itself, universities and schools were bursting their seams with students and tidy, well-behaved children, often working three shifts a day to deal with the numbers.

Somewhere in all that, a private, vivid, purely Kazakh or Kirghizia dream of the future might still be hidden. I would not be surprised if it were so, but I would be surprised if it were not a diminishing one. The ardors of nationalism seemed already weakened in this great land tucked up against the mountains in the far-off heart of Asia.

From Kazakhstan I flew back to Tashkent, the capital of Uzbekistan. Seen from the air, in daylight, the city was like a bigger version of Alma-Ata: with a population of over a million it is twice its size. But on the ground, the imprint of Manchu and Mongol seemed fainter; that of Indian and Persian, Afghan, Turkoman and even Tibetan seemed bolder. Above all, the influence of wasteland and desert, and of the uncompromising state of mind and spirit that went with them, was strong in the air — and in the unevasive eye of the people. I saw more persons in national dress here than almost anywhere else in the Soviet Union. Even the man who rejected the full traditional white robe, which is cut low to expose the wearer's sun-burned chest, and wore instead a cotton shirt and worsted jacket, would still cling to the national skullcap, the *tibiteika,* embroidered in black and white patterns, as if to indicate that, whatever the appearance of the body, the head still was purely Uzbek.

Yet it would be a mistake to suggest that Tashkent wore only Uzbek colors. Here, mixing freely with the Uzbeks, come Kara-Kalpaks from

57

across the desert, as well as the natives of Kirgizstan and Tadzhikistan and many Asian regions beyond the Soviet frontiers. They turn the markets of Tashkent into gay, colorful and animated places. One knows at once that one is at a crossroads of geography, history and the spirit.

There is no doubt, however, who directs and controls this traffic: the master minds and hands are Russian. Life is more industrialized; the canals are longer, broader, and their gleaming sword thrusts pierce deeper into the vitals of desert and distance.

The show piece is the Russian-made Ferghana Canal. Broad as a river, it leads the mountain waters across the dry plains to feed what has become one of the most fertile regions on earth, the Ferghana Valley. Minor canals draw off water for fields of alfalfa and paddies of rice, and the water is protected against evaporation by great mulberry trees. There are orchards of apricot and peach trees, and melons grown to bursting strew the ground in between. And, of course, there are vineyards, the vines bent double with the weight of grapes which taste of muscat and press into wine worthy of Omar Khayyám.

Above all there is cotton. More than three fifths of all Soviet cotton is grown in this part of the world. Even the remote Hungry Steppe, the Golodnaya, is now a great cotton center, and each year Tashkent produces miles and miles of garishly printed goods for the rest of the country.

Important, however, as all these aspects in life made Tashkent, I thought its natural function as a meeting point and transformer of many cultures and minds was perhaps greater. This may have been the reason the Comintern chose it as the location of one of its main schools of world revolution before the war. Today Tashkent has become one of the most important centers for legitimately spreading Soviet influence by providing free education for young people from all over the world.

Yet one night I walked out of a performance of the local ballet at the first curtain. I had already on other nights seen a circus, an opera and a theater and been to a palace of culture. These had been endured as a duty —

even the opera, which was Russian and melancholy to the point of parody, with character after character giving strange satisfaction to the audience by jumping into the Dnieper River on the last echo of a prolonged outpouring of outraged soul. But the ballet was too much. It was thinly based on the life of Strauss. The superrefined sentimental evocation of Hapsburg Vienna, the golden-syrup rendering of Strauss' music, the costumes and décor as real as illustrations in a book of nursery tales — all these combined were too much for me.

I went out feeling as if I had been fed on pink marshmallows and white cotton candy. The walk along the wide streets, generously lined with trees, past somnolent white houses with orchards, and the astringent air of early spring coming down from the thawing snow on the mountains, soon brought me back to my contemporary senses. I was beginning to be aware of some of the limitations of the Soviet concept of self-determination for its subject races. The national ballet I had seen was folksy to an alarming degree. The prudery of local palaces of culture, where girl dancers wore long pink slips tied by elastic around their ankles so that their legs would not show when they twirled, I could hardly take as a sign of emancipation. The pernicious anemia of it all contrasted strangely with the vigor one met in education, agriculture and industry.

From Tashkent I flew south and west to visit the storied cities of Samarkand, Bukhara and Ashkhabad. On the way the sun became hotter, the dry steppe merged quickly into the desert proper, and the earth became sand which stretched west and northward as far as one could see. To the east and south the purple mountains still stood firm, flaunting a feather of snow in our faces.

But what excited my eyes and imagination even more were the desert and the narrow chain of fertile oases that connected the few mountain passes with routes to the Caspian and other worlds beyond. There lay the great silk route, one of the bloodiest thoroughfares of all time, which began in

China and linked up here with other trails to Persia and the Middle East, Byzantium and the Levant, and the unborn countries of Europe.

One of the greatest fallacies of our way of telling history is the unconscious assumption that exploration on any significant scale is a European development started in the fifteenth century. But the urge to know the unknown, to learn what is not yet learned, to submit the old and the outworn to rejuvenation by the new and the untried, to trade and to travel and at the worst to convert and to conquer, is built into the spirit of man and was present and active at our beginning.

The past still lies heavily on Samarkand and Bukhara, and in the spirit of their native-born people. In these two cities there is still more of the old than the new, and for this we have the Russians to thank. Once they were convinced that they had no revival of nationalisms to fear, they set out with a powerful will to preserve all that is best in old Samarkand and Bukhara. They have even put craftsmen to work in the cloisters and cells of many mosques, using the same methods as their prototypes of the Golden Horde, to produce tiles of the exact shade to replace the broken and missing ones. Had they not done so, there is no doubt these cities of sun-baked brick would have crumbled fast.

I myself first saw Samarkand from a rise across the wilderness of crumbling ruins and great graveyards that lie along the road from the airport. Suddenly we caught a glimpse of painted minarets trembling in the light, and the great blue domes of mosques and tombs shouldering the full weight of the sky among bright green trees and gardens. I had a deep sense of coming into contact with one of the most astonishing cultures in history, the world of the one and only Allah and his Prophet Mohammed, whose teaching lives on in the mind and spirit of Central Asian men.

The building that moved me most was the Gur Emir, the blue-domed tomb of Tamerlane, and the plain tombstone of jade from China which marks where the great conqueror now lies in his small coffin. The whole city still speaks of this extraordinary man, Timur the Lame, and of his grandson Ulug-Beg, the great astronomer.

Yet the memory of Samarkand which stays with me most clearly was more humble. On my last evening there, coming back to the city from the country, we passed some unusual elms and I stopped to look at them. They were, my guides told me, perhaps a thousand years old, older certainly than Genghis Khan. It was very still, and the mountains away toward Persia were purple, white and pink in the declining light. A flock of fat-tailed sheep tended by some Tadzhik children moved slowly homeward in the distance, leaving a trail of yellow translucent dust in the air. Then from the city came quite clearly the call to prayer from mosque and minaret, and beyond the trees an old man dismounted from his donkey, spread a prayer mat on the ground, kneeled down facing Mecca and began to pray.

No one who had not traveled in a country without gods in the religious sense can know how moving such a scene can be. My companions, however, were oddly embarrassed. "Some of the old people," one of them said, "are still very superstitious, but we'll soon change all that." And he laughed.

His laugh drove all feeling of reverence out of the evening, and afterward the night over the domed and painted city seemed all the darker.

A bare generation ago, Bukhara was perhaps the least changed of all the cities of Uzbekistan. It was still contained within its white walls and towers, but the walls now have been pulled down — to let air into the place, the Russians say. Today, at what used to be one of the richest market places in the world, one buys ice cream instead of slaves, mass-produced trinkets and fizzy drinks instead of opals, diamonds, gold, lapis lazuli, and turquoise jewelry. Few of the four hundred mosques remain, and most have vanished without a trace. One is now a popular billiard parlor, another a palace of culture. The Liabi-Khans, the beautiful tree-shaded pool in which the three hundred wives of one emir used to perform their evening ablutions, is an unofficial swimming pool for street urchins.

Yet enough of the past remains. The Kok Gumbaz or Blue-Domed Mosque and the vast Mir Arab in the center of the city still stand, and everywhere there are walls of red and yellow bricks covered with algebraic arabesques like maps of the profound and intricate Moslem spirit. The Zindan, or prison, the death pit in which the emirs kept snakes and scorpions to torment the men they threw in, the Tower of Death from which the condemned were hurled — these and other historic structures survive.

At Ashkhabad, the capital of Turkmenia, a region the size of Spain and of nearly two million people, the mountains of the Persian frontier were a bare twelve miles away and the desert seemed to press right up against their base. The low white houses of the town, built in wide green avenues, repeated the pattern of other Central Asian towns, but the people had now changed subtly. There was more evidence of temperament: I walked into my hotel to find a waitress and a waiter shouting at each other because one of them had laid a table badly. My relief after so much averted and hidden spirit, not to mention Russian conformity and phlegm, was immense.

Some of this vividness was reflected in the people's clothes and in their arts and crafts. It seemed no accident that red was their favorite color. I saw many men in dark red gowns and great black fur hats, and women in flaming dresses of deep red, with silver ornaments flashing against their olive skins and dark hair. Even the younger ones who wore modern clothes did so with a clear sense of style and taste that I had not seen before. The background of their beloved carpets was likewise red, and I do not believe I have ever seen so many beautiful shades.

Neither in Samarkand, Bukhara nor in any town in Persia, the locals claimed, did they make carpets as fine as in Turkmenia. They took me to the local factory to prove their point — and first off they showed me proudly one girl weaver who was a Heroine of Soviet Labor, an honor which is to the new Soviet worker what the Victoria Cross and the

Congressional Medal of Honor are to British and American servicemen. This girl, I was told, produced more than twice as many carpets as any other girl in the factory. Now all the girls I had seen up to this moment were working steadily and easily at their weaving, occasionally pausing to talk to one another and not afraid to satisfy their curiosity by thoroughly looking me over. But this Heroine of Labor did not pause once. I spoke to her and she did not seem to hear. Head bowed over her work, fingers passing threads of different colors through the frame in front of her as fast as they could, her eyes moving in the hypnotic way of spectators at a tennis match from one end of her pattern to the other, she seemed living not in the present or in the past but far off in some insect form of life.

To me this seemed a frightening denial of life in so comely a young girl, and I asked, "Does she do this all day?"

"Oh yes, from the time she comes in until she leaves," the manageress replied with pride as she took me away to show me the stock of carpets.

A melancholy settled in me as my plane headed westward toward Baku, but presently I was relieved to see the greater and lesser Balkan hills come out of the plain, and beyond them the glint of the waters of the world's largest lake, the salty Caspian Sea.

As we approached Krasnovodsk, the busy port and railway terminus on the eastern shore, an important-looking Armenian beside me pointed out a lesser glint of water on the northern horizon, apparently detached from the greater. That was the strangest of all Caspian subwaters, I was told, the Kara-Bogaz-Gol or Black-Mouthed Gulf. Once not long ago the Caspian used to flow through the narrow entrance which links the two, replacing the vast quantities of water lost through evaporation in the smaller, desert-locked lake. But the Caspian itself has been falling rapidly, and today the shallow Kara-Bogaz-Gol has to be fed by water pumped into it from special reservoirs.

What, I asked, if this steep fall in the level of the Caspian continued?

His dour, dark features came close to a smile and he answered that Russian scientists had evidence that the fall was cyclical and would in time be followed by a rise. Yet even if it were not, a plan already existed to deal with the problem. Did I know that not far from the source of the Volga, which was the Caspian's greatest source of supply, rose other great rivers whose waters flowed northward and added only to the superfluous ice in the Arctic? They were going to turn these rivers around, force them back into the catchment areas and tributaries of the Volga, and so make them flow into the Caspian.

As he spoke of these rivers and what Soviet man would do with them, he got in his eye what I came to call the "river look." All the Russians I met had it, but it was so intent on some faces, particularly those of hydroelectricians and river experts, that it was just a little mad. There seems to be a profound electricity mystique in the Russian soul, as if they believed this form of energy to be a miracle that will not only transform man's physical being but also insure his spiritual transformation and ultimate salvation from evil. Accordingly, I found myself thinking of a charming story told by Vera Imber, famous as the woman poet of Leningrad's gallant fight against Hitler. In this story she tells of a visit paid by his grandchildren to a cultured Greek of the old school in Odessa, a city of great cultural traditions.

"And what is your little brother's name?" the old gentleman asked his young granddaughter when she arrived.

"Rem," she replied.

"Ah! short for Remus," he replied, thinking of Uncle Remus.

"Nothing of the sort," the terrible new world child replied. "It stands for Revolution, Electrification and Metallurgy."

Now my Armenian companion poured out all the information he had about the world over which we were flying. He spoke of the great fishing industry in the Caspian, with its centers at Astrakhan and Bakum of mullet, sturgeon caught for food as well as for caviar, bream, pike, skate and a migratory fish which spawns in the rivers and then returns to the lake. Seal fishing, he said to my astonishment, was an important occupation in the northern Caspian, where they were caught on the ice in winter. Yes, despite the glare and the heat around us here, it could be bitterly cold in the north.

We were over the Caspian by now, and its green-blue surface went blue and then almost black. Just where we were now, he said, halfway between two shores (both, at 30,000 feet, nearly out of sight), the sea was more than 3,000 feet deep.

Soon, however, the shallows came, and with them a new excitement. We saw the oldest oilfield in Europe extending right into the sea. From the land, the giant derricks strode like pylons far out into the waters. My companion talked of this underwater drilling for oil as a purely Soviet invention. It was remarkable how even so educated a man seemed to have no worldwide point of reference. His one unfailing comparison was with conditions in Imperial Russia before the Revolution. But he was a sensitive, almost poetic observer of nature and I was sad to part from him at Baku.

Both the land and the oilfields outside Baku looked their age. The land for miles seemed bare, wrinkled and worn out with time. The pumps on the wells, already more than ninety years old, drew up oil from great depths, their pistons moving with the slow, trancelike motion of things near the end of their days.

Then, as I neared the city, the earth seemed to revive. It was covered with yellow flowers, grass appeared on the dunes, trees full of light and color came into view. My guide told me that every year more and more of the sterile earth along the Azerbaijanian shores of the Caspian, the territory of which Baku was the capital, was being redeemed. Like all the Azerbaijanians I met, he was intensely proud of Baku. This intense metropolitan consciousness was new to me. It suggested a move toward the West in the spirit of man, away from the Central Asian attitude.

It was remarkable how much of a sea atmosphere lay around the shores of so land-locked a water. My first day there was a Sunday, and in the evening the esplanade was crowded with sailors in neat dark-blue uniforms strolling about with girls on their arms. And the people as a whole had something of the gaiety and lightheartedness one associates with a sailor ashore. I spent an evening at the palace of culture of the Union of Seamen; if I had shut my eyes I could have believed myself in an audience in Marseilles.

It was all a fresh revelation of the Mediterranean world as a whole. The ancient affinities between the Pillars of Hercules and the Hellespont are more valid today than many of us realize, and they create a unified temperament and attitude to life. Whether an individual calls himself Greek, Turk, Levantine, Arab, Tunisian, Spaniard, Provençal, Italian or Dalmatian, he is also someone who makes sense only when conceived of as Mediterranean man. This southwest shore of the Caspian was consciously and in every demonstrable way part of the Soviet Union, but there was no doubt in my mind that by instinct and intuition its loyalties were slanted the Mediterranean way.

Largeness of gesture was implicit in the man of this world, and in Baku I had to learn to be careful even in asking the way, for many people would go to great trouble to take me to my destination themselves, or else put me on the appropriate streetcar and try to pay my fare.

To add to this Mediterranean sense, the waiters at my hotel now addressed me in French. I would sit by a window in the restaurant, looking over the broad bay and watching with envy the fat Caspian steamers sail out for Astrakhan, Balykshi, Krasnovodsk and other parts of Russia to which I was denied access, and have long talks with the *maître d'hôtel* about French literature. Flaubert was his favorite author and *Salammbô* his favorite novel. The historical novels about the ancient Mediterranean world were his preference, he told me with animation and many a colorful gesture. The tide of individual temperament, for which I had listened in vain on this long journey, was now active and audible in him and others. There was a sea within as well as one without: and this was not a bad preparation for Georgia.

66

III

Georgia and the Black Sea Ports

My first impression of the crowded airport lounges at the capital of Georgia, Tbilisi (as the 1,500-year-old city of Tiflis is now called), was that the men in it were taller than any I had yet met, and the women taller and straighter. Both sexes appeared refreshingly unself-conscious and looked one straight and boldly in the eye. The voices of the men were as deep as their valleys and as animated as their rivers, and they talked, laughed and joked incessantly. Here the tide of temperament which I have mentioned spoke in the sound of a high sea swelling and making urgently for the shore.

Years ago, in talking with W. E. D. Allen, who has written perhaps the best English work on the history and people of Georgia, he had spoken of them as close to the Irish in temperament and had used a phrase that came back to me now: "the aesthetic irresponsibility of the Georgians." I remember his saying that the Georgians and the Irish were the only people who ever fully realized the positive creative uses of irresponsibility. The Georgians refused to take their conquest seriously. They remained their laughing, gay, unchanging and unchanged selves, not stopping for a moment to confer dignity on their conquerors.

Out of this attitude, as with the Irish, grew a certain disdain of forethought and prudence, and although many an alien creed and system came and went, the Georgian and his quicksilver temperament remained. I stress this here not only because it shows how much nearer I had drawn to the

Mediterranean world, but because henceforth I was to find that all the minority peoples who have been bound to Russia, either as integral parts of the Soviet Union or as satellites, had evolved techniques of their own for denying their conquerors.

Meanwhile I enjoyed myself hugely in Tbilisi and the country round about. I longed to see some of the isolated peoples of Georgia — the two villages of Negro Caucasians, for instance, and the gallant tribe of Ingush, who only twelve years ago were still reported to be skirmishing with the Russians. Alas, I was told such a trip was impossible, so the best I could do was to go some eighty miles by car along the great Georgian military highway into the mountains. The beauty and variety of the scene were great. As the sea moves us by its sameness, so these mountains and valleys moved me by their infinite variety.

In the valleys it was already spring; wheat, barley, oats were sprouting green, their blades precise and erect in the dark earth. Peach, apple, cherry, apricot and plum were in flower, and against the giant mountains the blossoming looked poignantly delicate and tender, clinging like rainbow vapor to the trees. Cattle, fine-drawn by winter, grazed up to their ankles in new grass, and from time to time we met flocks of sheep feeling their way toward the mountains to follow closely the retreat of snow from the rich, high summer pastures. Many of the shepherds were exceedingly tall, and wore Caucasian tunics down to their knees, daggers at their belts, silver-clasped cartridge cases on their chests, soft high boots, and capes flung back like a challenge over their shoulders.

Sometimes I would get out of the car to examine a church or a ruin, and always I was amazed at the richness of the past that remained in them, at the Byzantine mosaics and frescoes left on the crumbling walls. A ford that Roman legions used to cross was pointed out to me, also a road followed by Pompey the Great.

On the way we stopped at Gori because I was curious to see the museum which had been made of Stalin's birthplace. We found his shrine, recently one of the most sacred in Soviet Russia, out of grace and favor. In Stalin's day the attraction of the museum, of his cobbler father's house and workshop, was so great that an enormous hotel was built in the vicinity to cope with the numbers of devout Communist pilgrims and tourists who visited it. Now the portentous hotel was empty, dank and gloomy. The museum and Stalin's home were both shut, it was said for repairs. There in his birthplace, in the land where fierce and stubborn loyalties might have been active to preserve his memory, this seemed the last fatal indignity.

A day or two later I came to the other Georgia, the Georgia which stretches along the Black Sea coast. Coming down through the pass and the broad valley in which the airport of Adler lies, I found it difficult to relate the one with the other. Away to the north the mountains were purple and the snow yellow with distance, but here, running down to the sea, they shook themselves free of snow and of all association with the Himalayas. The air became moist and mild, and a mixture of subtropical and temperate vegetation between the sharp slopes and the sea became as bewildering as it was fecund and tall.

The Russians have been so impressed by the extraordinary richness of their vegetable kingdom on the Black Sea that they have a fully qualified agronomist as head of their tourist bureau at Sochi. I believe this appointment, and the official attitude which occasions it, to be unique. I cannot imagine any other government or travel organization detailing a scientist to instruct tourists in the facts of the botanical life of their land. The arrangement, I suspect, was wasted; the tourists I met had other priorities in mind, and though few could have failed to enjoy the lavish vegetation, they were not interested in a technical breakdown of their impressions. The Russians who were aware of this must have found it a symptom of the levity and irresponsibility of the bourgeois world, but happily the majority never noticed it.

For me, nevertheless, the presence and function of the agronomist were another indication of how genuine and profound is the Russian respect for knowledge. Under the new order, many are so conditioned that they can never pass up an opportunity for fresh knowledge. My guides and interpreters, whenever I used an expression they had not heard before, would immediately whip out their notebooks and make me repeat and explain it while they wrote it down.

The sense of a special mission to redeem life and save the world is potentially present if not active in most Russians today. They are a nation of missionaries.

Accordingly, the men in charge of an experimental citrus station on the sunny hillside above Sochi had named one of their largest experimental plants the Tree of Universal Friendship. All visitors of distinction — and these included numbers of well-known men and women from all over the world — were invited to make a graft of citrus on one of its branches. The head of the station, an elderly scientist with beautiful manners and an obvious love of his work, would himself show visitors how the grafting should be done. Then he noted their addresses, and thereafter his staff kept them posted annually on the progress of their particular experimental hybrid. The grafting done, each visitor was presented with a minute knife as a badge of his membership in the order of this tree. It had something of the symbolism of a religious rite, and I feel that it could happen only in Russia.

The Black Sea coast is great vineyard and market-garden country, but it is also great sanatorium country. The word is misleading to us. The Russians use it to describe not only hospitals and convalescent homes but also recreation and rest homes. For miles around the popular resorts, the immense sanatorium buildings stand shoulder to shoulder, and the time is approaching when this north coast of the Black Sea, from Batumi in the east to Odessa in the west, will present an unbroken front of concrete colonnades.

The warm climate, of course, makes the region a natural playground for people condemned to live through the full round of harsh seasons in the great interior. The State and the workers' unions have realized this, and the building of these accommodations has been given almost as high a priority as that of heavy industry. As a result, about 4,000,000 people spend their annual leave beside the Black Sea, almost one fourth of them in Sochi: and still the feverish work goes on.

Apart from the obvious natural attractions of the region, I believe that another, more subtle reason lies behind its development as a vacation area. This was once the playground of the aristocracy and the privileged classes of Tsarist Russia. Some of the villas and palaces they built, to occupy perhaps only a few weeks a year, still stand cheek to cheek with the mass-produced buildings of the new regime, and it is not difficult to imagine how the masses of contemporary Russians feel about them. To them, I think, one attraction of the Black Sea coast is that it offers a way of getting even with their appalling past.

When the agronomist took me into my first sanatorium, in the Matsesta Gorge outside Sochi, he waved his hand at it proudly and exclaimed, "A veritable temple of health, don't you think?"

I was interested in the phrase he used. The Soviet State may build no churches but it does build many kinds of "temples", from factories and railway stations down to the glorified boardinghouses on the Black Sea coast with their Greek columns and classical marble arcades. All these structures suffered an inflation of form in no way concerned with their functions but derived purely from the unemployed religious energies of a people who are naturally deeply religious. And the agronomist's "temple" was just the right word for the manifestation.

The beach was the only place where people could find themselves in a state of inactivity and oblivion, and this, I think, together with their long harsh winter, accounted for their utter abandonment to the sun. It is true that the State radio pursued them even there, its din resounding in that lovely setting. And there was more talk than music on the air: the dreary official exhortation, elucidation and indoctrination. But the people lying on those beaches, close packed for hundreds of miles, did not seem to hear a word. They lay there inert, wrapped in the sunlight as in a honey-colored blanket of Iberian wool.

Finally, besides being great holiday country, the Black Sea coast is also great "delegation" country. From Sochi on westward, the land was teeming with these carefully screened groups. I found myself traveling with the same delegations for days at a time, and without speaking to them I got to know their characters rather well. The Rumanians were the only delegates who seemed to be enjoying themselves; they could be as lighthearted and sparkling as the Georgian champagne so liberally poured into their glasses. The Czechs were perhaps the most serious, gravely pragmatic and determined to extract the most out of the situation. The Bulgarians seemed filled with lugubrious disillusion. Significantly, I saw no Polish delegations. I did meet several East German delegations, and I regret to say they had an extremely unpleasant effect on me. They appeared thoroughly ashamed of themselves, as if they knew what they were doing was wrong but did not have the courage to desist. They never looked either me or one another in the eye, and they ate in a way no human beings should be allowed to eat.

For a time one German delegation, a small party of Americans and I found ourselves repeatedly in the same hotels. The looks the Germans gave the unsuspecting Americans were filled with an animosity I could not understand. I mentioned this to the cultivated Russian woman who was in charge of the American party and whom I had got to know rather well.

"They do hate these Americans," she told me. "Can you guess why?"

"Because of the war?"

"Oh, no, nothing real like that," she said. "It is simply because the Americans always leave some food uneaten on their plates. The East Germans leave nothing on theirs and not even a crumb on the table. They think it wicked of the Americans and a sign of how spoiled and wasteful they are."

"They must hate easily then," I said.

At that she gave me a sharp look and asked with some tartness, "But don't you realize the Germans are a very dangerous people? Won't you, the French and the Americans ever learn your lesson?"

The delegations that disturbed me most were those of mixed international and professional Communists and fellow travelers brought together from all over the world. It was extraordinary how, though they came from different races and cultures, they all managed to have the same look. There was no joy in any of them. They ate and drank sparingly and hardly ever spoke. Words, one felt, were reserved for tracts and lampoons; speech for conferences. They would sit tight-lipped, not seeing the lovely earth glowing at the windows but only the scene of some implacable memory within.

I observed this so often that I realized as never before that what we loosely call Communism is a state of mind long before it emerges in the form of a dialectical materialism. Moreover, it is a state of mind that obsesses people who have never even heard of Marx, Engels or Lenin, and it can obsess many people who are fanatically opposed to the political Communism of either Russia or China. It is its existence in the world that makes Russia dangerous, not Russia herself. What Russia is does not imperil us, but what the world imagines Russia to be does imperil us. This fantasy can go so deep that it makes irrelevant all the contradictions, paradoxes, inconsistencies and bewildering changes of fronts which mark the individual behavior of those who profess Communism. All these can be freely exposed. Man can lie and deceive quite openly, as the expediency of the moment demands, because deeply there is the one predominant purpose of a highly charged and polarized mind which remains unchanged.

For this reason Communism as a social or political philosophy makes no sense to me. But conceived as abnormal psychology, it is full of a somber meaning. The quintessence of it, perhaps, is that the original love of life, of justice and of man which gave birth to Communism has long since been cast out and forgotten. In its stead is left only the shadow of the vanished substance of these creative urges, and abstractions of hatred so great that it makes man not only incapable of experiencing the reality of love but even of recognizing it when offered to him.

The Russians are not, I am convinced, a people naturally predisposed to hatred. Communism among them has definite roots in their own history but has little to do with the state of mind of which I am speaking, though they have had and still have leaders who are afflicted by it. But by now the Russian people have taken their proper revenge on history, and there are signs that they are at heart sick and weary of what is left of hatred in their society.

Even so, the distorted picture they have of the Western world and its intentions, and particularly of America, is alarming. The only really heated discussions I ever had with Russians were about the United States. They were inclined to accept whatever I said about Britain, out of a natural respect for the feelings of a guest. But about America they had no such reservations. Their attitude in that regard was ambivalent to a remarkable degree. They admired America more than any other country in the world, and at the same time they envied, disliked and feared it. No one I met ever made a secret of the national determination to surpass America's industrial and material achievements. The achievement of the greatest industrial output in the world seemed to be a matter of profound personal and national self-respect in the Soviet Union.

I liked Yalta best of all the Black Sea resorts. Wandering around the town on foot, I discovered with delight that, for all the Soviet-style building imposed upon it, its inner shape was essentially conditioned by its past. It had what Sochi lacked, a core and a population that were independent of the great tides of distinguished visitors, tourists and bemused and bewildered workers from the interior which ebbed and flowed through it with the seasons. What had made Sochi memorable for me was its noble sunlight and magnanimous earth. But Yalta was a small Mediterranean city with a character and a temperament of its own.

One evening, just as the sun was setting, I came down from the hills and the woods in which I had been watching a lovely herd of deer. Rounding a bend I caught up with a group I had met on the beach. They were strolling toward the town and talking with great animation, but on seeing me they immediately broke ranks and insisted on my walking in the middle with them. They had just been discussing modern music, jazz and rock 'n' roll. They wanted to know what we thought in Britain of a score or more of singers and contemporary composers, mostly Americans, of whom I had never heard. Their knowledge of even the very latest popular Western music astounded me, and whenever I had to confess ignorance of some pop-song writer or singer they could scarcely believe me.

Since I knew there was hardly a foreign record of juke-box music on sale in Russia, I asked the engineer among them how they managed to know all these tunes.

"Oh, we get them from our tape recorders," he answered.

"But where do your recorders get the music from?"

"From the Voice of America, of course," he said. Then he added, "It's the favorite music of most young people today. We have our own jazz, too, but personally I prefer American and English, though the French are doing some fine syncopated stuff too."

"How do you know that?" I asked.

"From the B.B.C. and Swiss broadcasts."

"But what about your own traditional and folk music?"

He made a slight face and told me that traditional music was all right in its place, at feast days and official celebrations, but that he and his generation had had enough of it. "I could murder the fellow who wrote that song about the Ukrainian and the towel his mother made for him," he added. "It's really terrible stuff. Not contemporary."

Toward the end of our walk, just before we reached the town, the young engineer put his hand on my arm and called out to his companions, "Listen! Please, listen!"

We stopped and listened. The Black Sea was bound to the darkening sky by a broad band of deep red. The tops of the hills behind us were purple, and in the black woods, now flooded with night, the nightingales had started to sing with clear outgoing voices. We listened and then, as we walked on, I found myself telling them of the attraction the nightingale had for our own poets. They asked for an example. Remembering their attachment to their own contemporary age, I rejected Keats and recited slowly and deliberately from "Sweeney Among the Nightingales."

"Ah, T. S. Eliot," said one young woman who was studying chemistry.

I could not imagine her counterpart in Britain or America recognizing a quotation from a poem by Pasternak or any other Russian poet. Even to recognize T. S. Eliot would have been unusual.

"You amaze me," I told her. "After all, your literary director, Fadeyev, used to say that if hyenas could use typewriters, they would write poetry like Eliot."

They roared with laughter, and one young man exclaimed, "Thank God, those days have gone for good!" It was the first time on this journey that I had heard anyone invoke the name of God.

Before I left the Black Sea coast for good, I flew to Odessa to sample a voyage in a Russian ship. My interpreter had volunteered to accompany me, since the ship would bring us both back to Yalta after an overnight run, and he was disappointed that we were not staying longer at Odessa. This ancient city has a great hold on Russian imagination, not only because of its role as a seed bed of the Revolution but because it had been for thousands of years a firm point of contact between the savage interior and the civilizations of the outer world. It has an unchanging predisposition to freethinking and culture. The vast pre-Soviet opera house (an imitation of its Viennese prototype) is still one of the first sights proudly pointed out to the visitor, and the city in its older sections carries the stamp of much good architectural taste, French and English.

After doing the rounds of Odessa with the help of a woman guide who spoke fluent French, seeing sanatorium upon sanatorium and the new Odessa surrounding and overtopping the old in exactly the same barrack-room style, I found myself increasingly impatient to get aboard my ship. Yet I was there long enough to enjoy the devious interior of the old city; to take the evening air with the thousands of men and women who crowded the pavements and streets after work; and to stand on the famous Potemkin steps looking down on the neat harbor, beyond which was anchored the Soviet Antarctic whaling fleet.

We embarked just before sunset. I was disappointed to see that our ship, a 20,000-ton liner, was not Russian built; the *auf* and *zu* on the taps in my bath suggested that it was part of German war reparations. But the crew, at least half of them women, were all Russians. I was the only foreigner aboard.

An officer stood on the quay at the bottom of the gangway collecting tickets. The crowd of passengers pushed and jostled a great deal, and the officer himself was often elbowed out of position and importuned and shouted at from all sides, but he never appeared irritated or moved even to exhort the crowd to order. Nor did the people lose their tempers in the crush, though I saw women with babies in their arms roughly pushed aside by burly men, and parcels and suitcases squeezed out of people's arms. I saw seven persons sent running back to their hotels for their tickets.

There were four classes of passengers in the ship. The captain in his cabin, over coffee and a box of delicious Russian chocolates, emphasized to me that the stratification was purely a matter of money. "As they pay me, so they travel," he said. Presumably, when the "state of abundance" is achieved, the classes of travel will be eliminated.

A little later, pacing up and down the deck before dinner, I saw old ladies with black shawls around their heads looking for a sheltered place for themselves and their bundles along the iron bulwarks. I saw them peering through the windows of the first-class dining saloon, where stewards in white starched jackets were laying the tables with lighted candles, sparkling cut glass for white and red wine as well as water, ornate table silver, and peaked napkins spotless as Arctic snow. Yet I was wrong if I imagined that the old ladies were resentful. The vision brought a look of joyful interest to their faces as they pointed out each detail and discussed it with surprise and animation. Had they shaken their fists, I would have found it less frightening.

Later still I saw them lying on the hard deck, heads propped against their bundles, sleeping more peacefully than I was to sleep in my deluxe cabin that night. And in the morning I could detect no anger in them over the glaring contradictions of the night.

Page 81 Setting-up exercises at the miner's sanatorium in Sochi, on the Black Sea; 82 Couple on Sputnik Beach on the Black Sea; 83 A bathing pavilion in Sochi; 84 Seashore relaxation in Sochi; 85 A vacationer on Lake Riza; 86-87 Horse herder in the mountain fog near Piatigorsk. He still wears the broad-shouldered Caucasus cloak; 88 Shepherds from the village of Mleti; 89 Sheep being driven through the Aragva Valley; 90 Farm wagon returning from the day's work in the rolling country at the foot of the Caucasus; 91 A Georgian cowboy leads his herd; 92-93 Shepherds on their way down from the high country in the fall. They have lived the summer in the caravan; 94-95 Farmers ride their horses through a cornfield at the base of the Caucasus on the horizon; 96 A Karachayevtzy mother and child return from the fields. They are members of one of the numerous small nationality groups in the Soviet Union.

IV

Rostov and the Ukraine

As one goes east and north of the Black Sea, into the old Cossack country, the cultivation grows more and more intense until the whole earth flattens out into a teeming, seemingly unending world of wheat, cattle and men. And in the midst of orchards, plantations and immense sweeps of farmland, great factory chimneys appear, smoking fast and full, like battleships steaming into action. Krasnodar, Armavir, Novorossisk and Tuapse stained the bluest of days with smoke.

Rostov-on-Don represents best, perhaps, how Soviet Russia has transformed the Cossack world. I came to it feeling a lively excitement. It was to be not only my first experience of a modern Soviet city but also my first meeting with a great Russian river.

Every day I would walk down the banks of the Don to the harbor and watch the big ships from upstream points like Volgograd (as Stalingrad is now called) and from Moscow itself. I would look over the broad, luxurious passenger ships that sailed along its hundreds of inland miles. They were as comfortable as any Channel steamer between Britain and France, and I would have gladly sailed out to sea in them.

I caught my first real glimpse of *chernozem*, the famous black earth of Russia, on the way from Rostov to Kharkov, a major city in the Ukraine. I have never seen more profoundly exciting earth. Even its blackness was not the color of negation but of the mystery of the great power of growth and rejuvenation with which it is charged. On that day the sky was packed with storm clouds, and the lack of luster and light should have made the earth darker. Instead it had a sheen upon it as the glint on a raven's wings, and where a shower of rain had left moisture, it had a positive midnight brilliance. Against it, a muster of river gulls looked like a fall of snow.

At first it seemed that this wide unity of plain and sky was too much to expect. I thought some hillock would be summoned to discipline the prodigal scene and call such an immensity of flatness and space to order. But always beyond the next horizon there would be more. The horizon itself was a perfect circle, as if it were nothing but the expanding circumference of a ripple started by a pebble in a dark pond, in which we were condemned forever to be at the center.

And as the plain unfolded, so did the great pattern imposed by man upon it. I saw, from the air this time, the vast new world of mines and industries in the Donbas, as the Russians call the Donets River basin, which contains some of the richest and best coalfields in the Soviet Union and was exploited even in tsarist days. It is a most impressive spectacle of chimneys, hills of slag and coal, factories and mills standing shoulder to shoulder for hundreds of miles surrounded by fields of grain. In comparison, the Ruhr Valley, the Black Country of Britain, the reeking North of France seem miniature.

With this vision of the two Russias side by side — industry and the plains — I arrived in Kharkov in the evening, in pouring rain. I was apparently the only foreigner in the hotel, partly because it was too early in the year for tourists and partly because this was the eve of the great May Day celebration, when people are supposed to have finished their traveling and to be firmly in position. It was not surprising, therefore, that the hotel's service bureau informed me that a place had been obtained for me on the distinguished visitors' stand at the May Day parade. Would I like to use it?

"Can a duck swim?" I answered.

"Can a duck swim?"

I explained the expression while out came several notebooks. Laughing, one man said, "You may have to swim like a duck to the parade if this rain goes on. We are sad that you should see our Kharkov like this."

From time to time I have had unusual hunches about the weather, and now I felt the sky was going to clear. I asked them, "Would you like it to be fine tomorrow?"

"Of course," they replied.

I said I knew a celebrated witch doctor in Africa whose particular specialty was weather control. Would they like me to send him a message and ask him to insure that the sun would shine the next day?

I said this jokingly and expected only a laugh, but they entered into my suggestion at once as into a completely new game. How would I get in touch with my witch doctor? Even if he had a telephone there was no time now for a long-distance call.

I tapped my forehead. "Depend on it," I said. "The sun will shine."

From then on they played the game with a touching mixture of flippancy and seriousness. For the rest of the evening, whenever they ran into me they would ask, with an eagerness that amazed me, "Have you been in touch? What was the witch doctor's answer?" And this made me realize another thing about Russia: how barren of fantasy are the Soviet mind and scene. Suddenly I felt sad that I had not brought Lewis Carroll and Edward Lear for them to read; they seemed starved for some fantasy in their lives. It is difficult at this distance to explain how much pleasure their reaction to my fooling gave me, and how important and hopeful an omen it appeared to be.

The parade was due to begin at ten in the morning, yet during breakfast at seven it was still raining.

Early as it was, the streets were full of people as we walked the mile or so to the parade ground. It was clear that, if solidarity was the purpose of the day's exercise, we were going to experience it. All the gray walls of the great gray dripping buildings along the gray wet streets were covered with red bunting and streamers and banners bearing slogans in white and gold.

As we came nearer to the parade ground, a kind of claustrophobia assailed me. I felt more and more as if I were walking into a trap. On the corner of every street security police, militiamen and soldiers stopped everyone, not only us, and checked through their papers before allowing them to move on. Then repeatedly we met lines of militiamen coming down the street almost shoulder to shoulder to halt pedestrians at unexpected points and scrutinize identity cards and other papers all over again. Why all this, I do not know, except that it must be in the nature of totalitarianism to be suspicious, to be vigilant against the resentments and frustrations it knows it causes.

Up to then, everywhere on my journey I had been favorably impressed by the small numbers of police or militiamen I had seen in the Soviet Union. I realized now that I had been naïve; suddenly they were out in battalions. Looking back down the broad street, I could at one time see five rows of police going like combs through the populace, and when I looked ahead another rank was advancing upon us.

European arrangements for the control of large crowds appeared unbelievably amateurish and casual in comparison with this. Every side street was blocked by dark green military trucks backed onto the pavements and right into the buildings, with no space between one vehicle and another. Each barricade was manned by soldiers. With each control point or rank of militiamen we passed, I felt another prison door had closed behind me.

My hemmed-in feeling was due also to the atmosphere I picked up from the crowd. The singleness of mood of the thousands plodding through the gray morning seemed to me stifling and threatening.

Then something happened to lighten my spirits. It suddenly stopped raining, and a beam of sun caught a scarlet banner high on a barrack block and held it like a searchlight until the gold on the hammer and sickle in the center glowed bright. The clouds were parting fast and the blue sky coming through calmly and evenly. By the time we arrived at the parade ground, in Dzerzhinsky Square, perhaps the largest city square in the world, the tops of all the buildings were steaming in the sun. The day, no one could doubt, was going to be sunny and hot.

"Your witch doctor has been as good as his word." My Russian companion put his hand approvingly on my shoulder.

The parade started after a short address delivered punctually at ten o'clock. Then the brass bands struck up, thousands of bayonets glittered and the march-past began. I expected the spectators on the stands to cheer when the first formation came past, but they remained oddly silent, despite the cheer leader who had taken possession of the loudspeaker and was exhorting them to cheer or applaud. What communication there was between spectators and soldiery remained mute, and this to me was far more fearsome than any cheering could have been.

And the march-past itself was not the least alarming aspect. Rank after rank went by with fixed bayonets, and the men were in such close formation that the bayonet points came just below the cheek bones of the men in the next rank. They marched in a markedly unseeing, ritualistic way, rather as if they were sleepwalking. This impression got exaggerated emphasis from the goose step into which they broke as they came abreast of the spectators' stand. This is perhaps the oldest step evolved by the male animal to shake the earth and make his enemies tremble. I know tribes in Africa who still practice it and indeed do it better and more elegantly than any Europeans, since it is still natural to them. Here it seemed a degrading way for civilized men to march, especially on a day devoted to peace and universal brotherhood.

After the soldiers came the athletes, followed by the Union of Workers. Then came the banners, all in red, and after them came photographs of the Communist great carried on poles — like icons in a religious procession. At last came the citizens, either arm in arm, or carrying sprigs of plastic flowers and bunches of colored balloons. Although the red flags still flew far and wide over the square, these balloons brought relief for the eyes in their varied colors.

Not until one o'clock did the parade come to an end. By that time, my Russian friend said, some 700,000 marchers had passed through the square (the population of Kharkov is about a million).

The experience, even at this distance in my memory, remains one of the ugliest I have ever had in peacetime, a reversion to a pattern of life which surely is discredited enough in all our histories.

I think this "ugliness" needs some elaboration. One of the paradoxes that gave me much trouble on my journey was the contrast between the delicacy, tenderness and sensitivity that I was aware of in conversation with the Russians I came to know best and the total absence of these qualities in the world they were making for themselves. They seem indifferent to the appearance of things and are able to see in objects only the reflection of what they long for in themselves. In a way they are all natural Don Quixotes with the power to convert every mill on the international skyline into a tyrannical capitalist giant, apartment blocks into castles in Spain, and Party bosses into saints. Only in music, it seems, is their taste infallible. But when it comes to the claims of visual realities they are incapable of meeting them. They are, on the whole, without a visual sense.

All Soviet towns, for example, have parks of rest and culture. I had been to many, and now here in Kharkov I realized that it was useless to expect them to change in character. They could vary only in size. The layout was always the same, and the statues were always the same. There would sometimes be one of Gorky, always in the same thoughtful pose, and always at least one of Lenin. I came to hate not the man but these statues and portraits of him. Every town and village had one; every railway station had at least one if not two; every official building had either a full-length statue, a bust or both, and above every desk of importance was placed an oil painting of Lenin in collar and tie. I was to visit one small station in Siberia where a statue of a skier was flanked by statues of Lenin, the only difference being that the first faced the world nonchalantly, hand in pocket, while the other with shoulders squared, clenched fists and raised arms pointed a naked finger to the empty steppe.

I was so bothered by this insect proliferation of the same Lenin image that one day I was trapped into exclaiming to a Russian companion: "You do have an awful lot of statues of Lenin about the place!"

Instantly he snapped back at me: "And why not? Aren't your towns full of images and pictures of Christ?"

I had only to think of the dynamic, infinitely varied role that Christ has played in the imagination of Western art to realize how wide the comparison was of the mark. I, however, dropped the subject at once. But the important point was, to me, that this cultured and educated Russian had seen an identical similarity between the meaning of Christ for us and the meaning of Lenin for him.

Leaving Kharkov for Kiev, I thought how wonderful it always was to get into the real country again. One's senses, that had become so narrowed and directed in the city, could now expand. For me there was an unfailing therapy in the view of the Russian plains.

Our arrival at Kiev, on the great Dnieper River, was no anticlimax. Destroyed in the war, rebuilt and expanded since then in standard patterns, it yet wears its conformity with a difference. This is due largely to its original situation athwart ancient trade routes and to its noble past as the enlightened capital of medieval Russia. This "mother of Russian cities" stands at the meeting of the two great roads of Russian history: the river road and that of the black earth.

Even today nothing about the city is small or mean. The streets are wide, and many have lanes of lime, poplar, chestnut, locust trees and gardens down the middle. The skyscrapers do not crowd the pavements but stand well back to give space, fresh air and quiet. Much has been preserved of what was good in the past. The same golden bubble domes I had left behind in Moscow again soared in the air among the modern apartments, looking strangely detached from their towers, as if floating like balloons up into the blue.

The great cathedral of St. Sophia, each wall, ceiling and pillar a vivid and crowded Byzantine mural or mosaic, has been superbly restored. The crowds visiting it were so dense that I had the greatest difficulty getting in and around the church. Here public interest in a cathedral was perfectly respectable because the edifice had been declared a historical monument. One went to see it not for religion but for history and art.

Fortunately there are also other churches preserved by the State. The Pecherskaya Monastery with its eleventh-century mosaics, although partially destroyed by the Germans, still has its gate-tower church, its wonderful bell tower, and a surprising number of other buildings and walls colored like pages torn from a Nestorian hymnal. The Andreyev church, built by the great Italian architect Rastrelli, who built so much of St. Petersburg, and his Russian disciple Michurin, adds something of the Renaissance to the prevailing Byzantine air. Kiev is fortunate, too, in preserving intact a lovely palace, also built by Rastrelli, and some romantic statuary from the past.

But most fortunate of all, Kiev possesses a hill with a remarkable view over the Dnieper. If I had thought the Don impressive, the recollection was instantly excelled by my first glimpse of the Dnieper. It is so wide and swollen that it is almost shapeless, and it swims over the flawless horizon in what looks like a succession of lakes. This is indeed a river worthy of so great a plain.

Wherever I looked across the river, new buildings and factories were springing up beside what was already a compact town of tall chimney stacks, mills and power stations. The feeling of long-pent-up and unused energies released and flowing in the wide bed of a concerted plan was as tangible as the view of the massive river making for the sea. There was little smoke in the air, for enormous reserves of natural gas have been discovered below this ancient black soil, adding to Russia's already rich supplies of oil, black coal and "white coal," or hydroelectric power. I was to learn that even Riga, on the Baltic hundreds of miles north, cooked its meals and warmed itself on gas from the Ukraine.

Only fools would ignore the formidable implications of such a vision. The Soviet Union is at the merest beginning of its industrial development, vast as that beginning already is. What will happen to the land in the process, what price will be paid in the values and meaning of life — these are other matters. Superstitions of the mind and spirit are bad enough, but the superstition about matter and machines which the Soviet State is putting in their place is, I believe, more deadly. Yet when I saw the Donbas I was certain that the greatest single industrial nation on earth was in the making before my eyes.

One day, remembering that some of the bloodiest struggles of the war had swayed back and forth across these plains, I asked my guide if I could see a military cemetery. I imagined that, after such slaughter, there must be many. At once she took me back to see the Eternal Flame burning in a granite, stereotyped war memorial. I shook my head and explained what I wanted to see, but she became somewhat confused. Finally she declared that this monument was for all the dead, and surely it did not matter to the dead whether they were buried individually or collectively! Surely nothing mattered to the dead once they were dead.

I did not try to explain.

Naturally, on these battlefields, I asked my companions about the war — which is always referred to as the Great Patriotic War. In measure I could understand that. I think the Soviet Union came of age during the last war. For the Russians it was a terrible initiation into the contemporary world, and they naturally put its profound national consequences first. At the same time it is extraordinary how little the plain people (not those who have to deal with foreigners) know about the war elsewhere and about the part that France, Britain and America played in it. I read articles by military "experts" who gave the impression that Russia, save for some gallant Czech, Rumanian and Yugoslav Communist partisans, fought and won the war alone.

The great plain, which in the south seems so level, began to undulate as we went farther north toward Moscow. The earth itself grew grayer, towns and villages became fewer, woods, copses, forests and marshes multiplied until one was quite startled by the sight of a factory, the TV aerials of a village, or the blue bubble dome of some decaying church spire rising above the trees. Roads were few, untarred and rough, and had a disconcerting knack of vanishing abruptly into the woods without apparently leading anywhere. Each stretch of cultivated earth, each village seemed unconnected with any other. Deep here in western Russia, it was astonishing how empty was the landscape and how slight upon it the impression of man.

But there was an abundance of woods, marshes and rivers — those in the forest stained tobacco-brown with the essence of peat. Each smaller stream joined a bigger one over a mouth of shingle waste until, around an unexpected sandy bend, it found the main river, broad and smooth, filled with light and cloud and blue sky, which was to take them all on together to the sea. Always it was a scene painted in subtle, limpid water colors. There were no hills, but we saw occasional red-sandstone cliffs or outbreaks of granite with deep ravines and gullies cut out of the gently undulating earth by water, wind and ice.

Both forest and cleared earth became increasingly green. Since I had first arrived in Moscow the spring had advanced in a rush. The flowers were vivid and profuse. Wood anemones, violets, celandine, cowslips, Solomon's seal, yellow globe-flowers and wild orchids, apple and cherry blossoms, and particularly the trailing bright bird cherry, all were bursting into flower together. I saw children in the villages staggering as if drunk on the scent, their arms full of lilies of the valley. I saw sturdy young girls, with shoulders like athletes and muscles like gym instructors, walking home behind the cattle with flowers in their hair, their belts and their hands. The softness in the spirit of nature, so ready to make generous amends for the ice and snow of the long winter, was most moving. I had expected the earth to be vast, rough and tough and was not prepared for such a flowering and so lush and tender a spring.

Then there were the birds — not just the small singing species vibrating like electric bells among the leaves and shadows, but game birds of all kinds, forest fowl clucking and whirring like bamboo rattles in sudden flight, and ducks and geese afloat on bronze lakes. Above all there were the white swans skimming the treetops, wings beating the silent air so fast that they resounded like some magic harp plucked into a passion of sound. I had never imagined that there could be such huge flights of swans outside the fairy tales of the brothers Grimm. They would fill the dawn and twilight hours with magic, and the woods with witchcraft.

I was much tempted to linger and go deeper into such country, but I had to go on to Moscow to attend to the shape of my remaining journey. Even so, the transition from such a natural scene to the artificial, regimented, inflexible capital was so sudden and brutal that I felt almost physically hurt by it.

The only consolation was that the efficient young lady in charge of my journey had not been idle in my absence. The authorities were now prepared to grant me permission to go by rail to Irkutsk, deep in Central Siberia, and by air to Khabarovsk, near the eastern edge of Asia. Because the airport at Irkutsk was under repair, I would have to return the five days' journey by train to Moscow and then fly back to the Far East. I had been long enough in the Soviet Union to accept this apparent illogic, and I spent no more time in Moscow than was necessary to complete the arrangements. Even so it took four days — and that, I was assured, was fast work — before I could get myself on the Moscow-Peking Express, which makes perhaps the longest rail journey in the world.

V

Central Siberia and the Far East

In the Soviet Union the train is not only a vital means of transport but also a thing of wonder in the popular imagination. Everywhere else in the world, with the exception of Japan, railways are increasingly dishonored, but here they are expanding vigorously. In all the thousands of miles I traveled by train in the Soviet Union, I never saw a vacant berth or a decaying railway station — indeed the stations are built and maintained like temples. The Yaroslave Station in Moscow, the terminal for train traffic to and from Siberia, was not the brightest architectural example of its kind, yet in other ways it was the most interesting, for it was a human marshaling yard of all sorts of men and women. Night and day it was full of people camping not only in the waiting rooms but out in the open, against the walls and the surrounding barriers. They apparently found nothing strange in being parked there like nomads in the heart of one of the world's great capitals, waiting for the appropriate mechanized caravan to take them on and out into the Siberian blue.

On my way to my train, which was to leave at twenty minutes past midnight, I had to step carefully through the numbers of campers. At first the platform was empty, but slowly it began to fill up with groups of twos and threes. Then suddenly a large Chinese contingent appeared in our midst. Most of them were civilians, dressed in Mao Tse-tung tunics, with cloth caps on their heads and the colorless raincoats of the new China on their arms. But at their center marched a compact little group of Chinese military, khaki capes to the ankles and bright insignia flashing on their collars and caps. It was extraordinary how they had the subtle, infuriating knack of making all else around them look untidy and chaotic.

There was one officer among the Chinese, a staff colonel, who held my attention in particular. He wore his uniform with remarkable elegance even for a Chinese, and he had a beautiful face. Then suddenly he moved, and the movement set something glittering below his ear. I could not resist going nearer until I could see distinctly that he wore long diamond pendants in his ears. I had hardly established this when I realized that this officer was a woman, for a black, shining braid of hair hung down to the small of her back. The difference between the new China and the old, which not long ago bound the feet of its infant girls to keep them small, seemed infinite.

My own sleeping car in the train was Russian-built but staffed by Chinese. I have never been in a roomier train; the Russians use the widest track in the world and thus have the broadest coaches. I had hardly entered my compartment when the Chinese attendant brought me a cup of tea made in the incomparable Chinese way, showed me how the lights worked, asked me what time I wanted to be called, and before leaving turned on the radio for me. Chinese music immediately filled the air and from then on was always on tap until I left the train five days later. Most of the train played Russian music but all the way to Irkutsk this coach, and the one behind it with the Chinese mission in it, broadcast only in Chinese.

My bed was already made up. The blankets were part wool, part cotton, the sheets and pillows of coarsish cotton, poorly bleached but fresh and spotless. I got into bed and turned off my light. I had barely time to think that I had never traveled in so smooth a train, not even in a California-bound express, when I fell asleep.

Morning came with the Volga at my window, nearly a mile wide and full of traffic. From the dining car I watched a great day expand over the countryside. I was alone except for two sturdy waitresses — Siberian travelers, I was to find, dined whenever their stomachs moved them, but all breakfasted late — so I could change my table from side to side at will and enjoy uninterruptedly what I saw. A light mist was dispersing from the hollows beyond the river banks and a landscape of incredible delicacy was coming into view. The woods and forests were of fine-drawn larch and birch sparkling in the light, with glimpses that were pure Corot. The marshaled brick and concrete of Moscow was gone and in its stead stood villages of wood, log cutters' huts with split logs piled high against walls that shone in the sun.

The fields were full of men and women working side by side. In the village streets were hens and chicks, ducks and ducklings, and the largest white geese I have ever seen. It was a scene in which nearly everything was wood and earth: nature was tender and delicate, but the detail imposed on it by man was rough and casual. No street or road was tarred, and all were uneven, full of mud and puddles, often ending up in bogs and ponds.

The domes and spires of old churches still stood, the greatest among them restored and splendid. Those within view of the railway track were dilapidated and forlorn, like molting hens, but visually they were a vital element in the scene. The villages and hamlets, gray and scarred by sun and frost, looked as if they had actually grown out of the soil. But if the shabby churches had not been there, earth and sky would have been greatly divided. The spires raised the vast earth and lowered the immense sky into a close embrace.

Page 113 A resident of Baikal gets his water from holes chopped in the ice of the frozen lake; 114 A boy in his Sunday best tests his fishing pole. He comes from one of the families that built the giant dam at Bratsk; 115 A springtime hike in Siberia for the children of the workers at Bratsk; 116-117 Fences delineate the private farming plots on the Lenin's Way collective farm on the road between Irkutsk and Baikal; 118 The giant dam at Bratsk; 119 A boy gathers frogs while standing on the logjam created by the diversion of the river at Bratsk; 120 A school teacher leads his young pioneers on a walk in the Siberian woods.

And in each window of the square little houses was the same vision of lace curtains neatly parted to expose the flower pot on the sill. The longing for refinement that these represented in that open setting was most touching. For many thousands of miles I passed through stretch after stretch of uninhabited land, but at each hamlet I would see the lace curtains and the flower pot, prim as ever, saluting the train as the mark of peasant self-respect. I can vouch that from European Russia to the Pacific Ocean there is not a window without a lace curtain.

At our first main station the train came alive with a rush. Chinese and Russian passengers tumbled out to pace up and down the platforms.

The Chinese civilians — their military contingent apparently had stayed behind in Moscow — were washed, shaved, brushed, manicured and neat in their tunics of blue. The Russian men, however, were almost all in pajamas, though their women were dressed in neatly cut blouses and skirts. I was to discover that most of the men wore pajamas all the time as a traveling suit, except in the dining car. Perhaps this display of male night attire was a badge of culture and emancipation, tangible proof that the wearers no longer slept in their clothes. Anyway, one fellow passenger, a Russian officer, seemed to find nothing incongruous in pacing every platform, all the way to Irkutsk, clad in green, yellow and purple stripes, with his military hat on his head and his war ribbons pinned on his pajama jacket.

At this as at all other main stops, the first people out of the coaches were the attendants, each equipped with a bucket and a mop on a long handle. They filled the buckets at the station main and washed down their coaches with great thoroughness. They would do this perhaps five times a day, with the result that our train glittered and shone. In addition it was cleaned within by powerful vacuum cleaners three times a day. I suspect that the attendants were kept so busy cleaning the train or making tea for the passengers that they had no time to make our beds. That we all had to do ourselves.

From midmorning until last thing at night the dining car was full and so was not of much use as an observation car. People came there not only to eat but also to shop, for one end of it was converted into a traveling trading post where passengers could buy such things as souvenirs, caviar, vodka, Ghanaian bananas and fine apples. The fruit was one of the great attractions but to me the prices seemed prohibitive. Innocently I bought a banana which cost me eleven shillings — more than a dollar and a half. But the other passengers, except the disciplined Chinese, bought the fruit in abundance until, at the end of the first day, only a solitary pineapple was left like a crown jewel in a case.

Then there were the shoppers from the forests and clearings, who immediately boarded the train at the stations for a spending spree. The farther east we went, the greater their numbers became, until finally the dining-car shop was so low in merchandise that it locked its doors to all newcomers.

The only people who remained apart were the Chinese. They would usually come into the dining car in a body and sit at their reserved tables. While eating they would talk only Chinese. They spoke to no one outside their group and no one tried to speak to them. This separateness was all the more striking because among themselves they were obviously gay, lively, sociable and entertaining people. They were, in fact, the happiest Communists I saw on my travels, and the nearer we got to China the greater their delight and the more exhilarated their behavior became.

At all the stations, fantastically long, slow trains were sidetracked to make way for our shining express. Many of them carried oil or industrial and construction materials. A great many were filled with passengers, and the traffic clearly was intense.

"The east is to us what the west was to the Americans," a Russian writer had told me in Moscow. "They used to say 'Go west.' We say 'Go east.' " And so the young of Russia are going east in their thousands. With them, too, go the restless, the misfits, the feckless, the footloose of all ages, streaming out of the more crowded west to the vast, wide-open spaces. I would see groups of hard-up young passengers at the stations, haggling with the saleswomen for stringy cooked chickens, hard-boiled eggs, bread, butter and sunflower seeds. Unlike my own traveling companions, they were not in pajamas but in track outfits and canvas shoes from their school and college days. For young people they were extraordinarily subdued and looked rather pathetic and overwhelmed.

Unfortunately, though we had many young children in our train, we had almost no young people. Our train was for the established and the respectable, not for the displaced and searching. The two young passengers we did have were hardly typical. They were, I thought, brother and sister. They were constantly in and out of the dining car. They appeared to have unlimited money and were the most expensively dressed persons on the train. Between visits to the dining car they would change their clothes. I did not see them wear the same clothes twice. They never spoke to anyone except each other, and they looked as if they despised the rest of us. It was not long before I was told that they were spoiled, a disgrace to society, had clearly never done any honest work or study in their lives, and must be the children of some powerful personage in the Establishment. What was the Soviet Union coming to!

In this way we swiftly approached the Urals. Kirov, a thriving industrial center of close on 300,000 people, held us only long enough for watering and the train's ablutions — and for a woman announcer to inform us over the loudspeaker that our train had just been taken over by "Locomotiveman Ryabov, leader of a heroic team of heroic Soviet labor and himself a hero of heroic labor." In his charge, she was sure, we would travel in comfort and safety, and she wished us all possible good speed on our journey.

Soon we were back in the country, and it was impressive how quickly the woods and forest closed in on us. By night we were at the entrance to the Urals. With little sense of increased altitude, we crossed the gentle and low ranges barely 1,300 feet above sea level. And in the dark, somewhere near the Chusovaya River, we flashed by the plain, striped post that marks the border between Europe and Asia.

I was up at first light and found myself in the gentlest of dawns looking at hills of pearl showing above woods of glowing red fire. For miles there was nothing but forest, streams that were mirrors full of cloud and sky, a lift of land like a mist above the woods. Then suddenly would come a new clearing, a peasant cluster of wooden buildings or a railway siding named The Peak or The Log Cabin, looking lonely and isolated. Others had names that spoke of their pioneer origin: Pancakes, Candle, Farthest Yet, Naked Boy Halt and my favorite, Studies.

Every now and then we saw women in felt boots and gray, dusty, worn overalls making heavy repairs on the track. I was to get used to seeing women working as hard as men in the Soviet Union, and often harder, but on this morning I found it a mournful sight. "Women and men," my Russian friends had told me time and again, "are truly equal only in Russia. Only here do they get equal opportunity of work and equal pay for equal work." But I remembered Blake's "one law for the lion and the ox is oppression." In practice it seemed to me that the women, whose nature also commits them to child-bearing, worked far harder than the men in Russia. That morning the faces that I saw beside the line looking up at us as we flashed by showed their indomitable patience, and also the look of rejection which is implicit in the absence of special recognition by their men and their societies; this look I know so well in the primitive women of Africa. Women also as a rule manned the wayside halts and sidings, wearing blue caps and blue serge coats and skirts. They would stand solemnly in pairs, holding up little gold flags as a sign that the way ahead was clear.

Where we halted now, I would find the indigenous Siberian travelers — the aborigines, as one Russian official called them — appearing in growing numbers. The shops, restaurants and waiting rooms were full of women in shawls, dark dusty skirts and woolen jumpers, and of bearded men in blouses and faded blue trousers tucked into mud-stained boots. The faces of both men and women were marked by sun, wind and frost. In their midst the pajamas of our train and the finery of the rich boy and girl seemed grotesque.

Yet these peasants were oddly indifferent to us. One felt they were no longer curious about men. They were curious only about what would come forth from the earth and the urgent harvest before the onset of their terrible winter. They saddened me greatly because they reminded me of my own Afrikaner people after the Boer War, all farmers too, poor, stricken and yet nobler by far than they are now that they have become rich and powerful. Yet there was nothing hopeless about these Russians. It just was that their hope lay in a dimension in which our twentieth century has no belief. I remembered an African proverb: "Patience is an egg that hatches great birds; the sun too is such an egg." That patience and wisdom lay like a clean garment upon these people. Why then did the sight sadden one? Perhaps because one was aware that one stood in the presence of people who are among the most profoundly rejected in the history of the world. The peasant in Russia has never been honored by the State nor given the share to which his courage, endurance and labor have entitled him. Even those who understood him best and were designed to love him most, like Peter the Great, found it convenient to exploit and betray him. Spengler, for all his sweeping generalizations, uttered some inspired truths about European history. He said that Moscow had no soul, that the spirit of the Russian upper classes was Western, and that the lower classes brought into the towns with them the soul of the countryside, but that between the two worlds there was no reciprocal comprehension, communication or charity. The last remark seems still to be true and the irony is all the greater when one considers that the peasants made the Revolution. The Revolution was already accomplished by the peasants and their soldier offspring when Lenin and his small band of professionals took it over. Yet their first priority was to reject the peasant. Lenin may have been a kindly person but he had no faith in or love of humanity. He loved only something called proletarian man and he and his successors one way or another have tried to change the people of Russia into this abstract image of human reality. This is one of the great differences between China and Russia. One of the first principles of Mao Tse-tung's revolution was to base it on the peasant and for this, among other reasons, I believe the revolution in China could prove ultimately to be more creative than the Russian one. In the beginning the Chinese avoided this fatal "apartheid" of the peasant which has made such confusion in Russian social and economic history.

When there was time, with this and similar thoughts in mind, I would leave the crowded station halls and walk into the villages and towns. It was curious how few of the other passengers did this, almost as if they were afraid of the space, the silence and the wide earth beyond. To me the villages, with their rough streets and duckboard pavements and square little houses straggling out into the blue, seemed even closer to the earth than I had imagined from the train. They clung to that dark earth for comfort and sustenance, and were the most moving thing I had seen thus far in the Soviet Union.

Back again in the train and speeding away, I would observe them grow smaller in their setting of sky and level plain, their beautifully plowed, raked and tended fields laid out around them like shining wet corduroy drying in the sun. Sometimes the peasants would be near enough for me to see them dropping pieces of potato into the earth, and at other times they were so far away that they seemed not to move at all. A horseman on the horizon, despite the dust smoking at his horse's heels, looked motionless in an aspic of space.

After such distances the towns always shocked one, and the first shock beyond the Urals was Sverdlovsk, a city of perhaps a million souls. It sat upon the earth like a giant tarantula in a web of railway tracks and wires sagging between the pylons. We were hardly halted in the vast, crowded, frantic station than our train was empty. It was extraordinary how a confidence, absent at minor halts and sidings, would return to the passengers at the smell of a city. They immediately became self-important, buying newspapers, writing post cards, drinking tea and showing off their pajamas.

In the Sverdlovsk station I felt a hand on my arm. I turned around. It was the man whom I had met — it seemed in another era — in the plane from Moscow to Tashkent and who had spoken to me so eloquently about his native land. I could not have been more delighted, and he, too, seemed pleased to see me again. He said he was on his way to Irkutsk, so now I had a friend of my own for the journey.

"Come on board and have some tea," he said, "and let us talk."

Quickly his love for his country came out again, and he seemed happy to talk to me about it. He begged me not to judge the 1,600-mile-long range of Urals by the gentle, delicate waves of land through which I had come. In the north they were higher and had a stern, rugged beauty of their own, and in the south their lush wooded grandeur was cataclysmic. He had just come to Sverdlovsk from the south along a track that had to twist like a serpent through the thickly wooded valleys, and on a blue day there was not a patch of sky without its eagle.

Below the cover of forest and grass existed a vast Aladdin's cave of the jewelry and lamp oil of nature. On the western slopes it was a world of oil, potassium, limestone and gypsum, and on the eastern of minerals easily reached: iron, chromium, manganese, nickel, copper, zinc, platinum, gold and precious stones. He wished I could see some of the gold areas, with their nuggets like hens' eggs, as well as the emeralds, amethysts, topazes, jasper, malachite, rock crystal, sapphires, garnets, tourmalines and aquamarines. Never, he stressed, has there been another country with such an abundance of mineral riches.

Already heavy industry in the Urals had an output far greater than that of all Russia in 1914. Thus progress in this region could now be taken for granted, and all the nation's creative planning be focused on Siberia and the Far East. Ah, Siberia — that story would out-fiction fiction! Siberia excited his emotions as had no other part of the land. I found that much of his youth and early middle age had been spent in working all over Siberia, even in the grim early years of the Revolution.

Did I realize that from east to west Siberia stretched more than 4,000 miles, and from south to north close on 2,000? More than 3,000,000 square miles of it was covered with forest — the *taiga*. In the *taiga* the summers were hot and short, the winters long. In winter the temperatures would fall to 70° below zero (Centigrade). Yet they were easily borne because the climate is dry and on the whole windless. Like all Siberians he was inclined to boast of the cold winters, yet he said that one Siberian summer was worth nine winters.

Surely, however, I could imagine the difficulties of surveying so vast a country in so extreme a climate? From above, the *taiga* was a sea of green that swept over plains, descended into valleys and broke over the mountains with equal intensity. Pines, cedars, silver firs, larches and spruces nearly shut out the sky. Many of the cedars were 250 feet high and nine feet in diameter. The moment a cloud covered the sun the forests were dark, and even in summer the poor geologist had a job finding his way around.

The worst forests were the black, damp coniferous ones on hilly and marshy ground. There the trees grew at all angles from the earth, and the space between them was littered with fallen branches and tops broken off by lightning. Working in these forests, how one longed for the great Siberian steppes, the southern plains or even the bare, cold and windy tundra in the north. Yet once out of them, one experienced a powerful nostalgia, found oneself longing perhaps to hear a great tree exploding like a bomb from the frost, and the tense wintry silence rushing in to wipe out the sound.

Then there were the swans, "the starlings of Siberia." One had not really seen swans until one saw them wild on these hidden *taiga* waters, ornamental as ever but so wild, vivid and passionate in their ways that the swans of Western Europe were shabby in comparison. Once when on an expedition and short of food, a member of his party shot a swan. All night long the bereaved mate flew round the camp crying pitifully for its companion. When dawn came and the dead swan still was absent, the other flew as high as it could into the sky and then at the peak of its flight folded its wings and fell like lead to its death on earth. It was, he said, deliberate suicide and he, for one, had sworn he would never again shoot a swan.

Again, he told me how he had flown over the place where the great meteorite had hit Siberia some hundred years ago. The place from the air was unmistakable. Suddenly there was this round space in the somber forest, a gleam of water at the center and row upon row of dead exploded or uprooted trees, bleached like cannibal bone, arranged like spokes around it in a perfect circle. It was an example to him of how remote and undisturbed Siberia was, that this graveyard of a star was lying there still so unchanged and inviolate.

Into this world geologists and scientists were sent by the thousands. Not only male geologists but hundreds of women, too, who roughed it with the men. The discovery of diamonds in Yakutia, for instance, was the work entirely of a woman from Leningrad. She not only evolved a brilliant new geological theory about diamonds but went out into the *taiga* for months and literally crawled about on her stomach to prove it. And prove it she did by discovering pipes of pure kimberlite, a mother rock of diamonds. The first pipe to go into production was, of course, named the Pipe of Peace.

As a result of this kind of searching and surveying, there was now in existence a geological map of the whole of Siberia, not only on the surface but down to 10,000 feet. What they had found was staggering: gold, tungsten, lead, zinc, copper and mercury. Siberia could supply the whole of the world with coal for two thousand years and still have some to spare. The new Siberian oil fields promised to be bigger than any of the older ones, and there were inexhaustible possibilities in hydroelectric power. The excitement, the belief in the future which burned in him was deeply impressive.

The one serious reservation in this theme of abundance had to do with agriculture. My companion was obviously concerned when I mentioned this, and he admitted it was a problem.

During the third night we reached Omsk, the town which in my imagination has always been typical of Siberia. By night it was just another busy station, and even on my return journey, when I saw it by day, it was just another large city on the Siberian plain. Both by night and day I thought I had never seen any place with so much sky and space around it. But now in the night, I saw immense thunderclouds moving out of the dark toward the sleeping city, resembling, in the spasmodic lightning, fabulous swans beating toward us on hissing wings of fire. I was awake for the rest of the night, and at dawn I saw the first slow river of the central Siberian plain uncoiling like a cobra out of the dark. A faint mist drifted over the surface, making the ripples caused by the rising fish look as if they were blowing smoke rings at the sky.

My first great Siberian river flashed into view only on the afternoon of the third day. It was the Ob, and I could hardly believe we were some thousands of miles from the sea, so full was it of traffic of all kinds, large passenger steamers, cargo ships, tugs towing barges and trains of lumber. On its bank, erect in a sulphur sun, stood the largely new city of Novosibirsk, already invested by an army of workers a million strong and its grain elevators proudly occupying the fords and riverbanks like Crusader fortresses. Scores of passengers left us here, for this is the strategic center of the new Western Siberia and the virgin lands, and other scores joined us. At the crowded station post office I would not have got my cables off had not a girl clerk spotted me for a stranger and insisted on serving me first.

Back in the speeding train, I watched the sinking sun raise a yellow gleam from a bend in the broad Ob, now gone bronze amid the blue of afternoon. Ahead of us I noticed a ripple on the earth which by nightfall increased to a wave. In the fading light the death of the great plain had an extraordinary personal impact on me. The earth was still black, but the farther we went, the more the woods intruded. Soon we entered a forest and my friend sighed: "Ah, a sample of the *taiga* at last."

The time I spent in Central Siberia and the Far East was the most enjoyable in all my journey. I felt more at home in these pioneering communities. The people seemed freer and more independent, and they tended to take the State less seriously and tragically. Their instinct was to suspect authority and to rely on their own judgment and capacity for helping themselves. I found them impulsive, rather reckless, open, quick-tempered and unbelievably generous.

Above all, they were proud of their country. Their pride made virtues of the grimmest necessities, and they boasted about their hardships in an affectionate way. They were convinced that their rivers, forests, lakes and plains had no equals in the world. And of course there were no Russians like Siberian Russians. Yet they were curiously unparochial. Indeed they were inclined to be in love with the unknown and consequently less suspicious of strangers.

My guide took me to meet a writer to whom I came to owe much. He was a poet just old enough to have been caught up in the last two years of the war. He was born in Irkutsk and assured me he would die there. He also wrote film scripts, and more recently, books for children. This last of his accomplishments interested me especially. I was continually struck by the proportion of Russian writers who have turned to writing fairy tales. It is, I believe, part of the revolt of their talent against stifling control by the State: a return to natural imagery.

"People," the poet said to me at one point, rather wistfully, "ironically barricade themselves against the nature that would save them. If they would only allow themselves to know it, they would find it full of wonderful things and power to help them. It is for that reason that I myself go to it and make certain that the imaginations of children, anyway, do not lose contact with nature."

It was characteristic of him that he was far more interested in showing me their river, the Angara, and its parent lake, Baikal, than the growing city of half a million people. So we set off for river and lake by car, with a chauffeur who likewise seemed typically Siberian. He was, my guide told me with some awe, pointing to a round colored metal badge in the driver's buttonhole, a Master of Sport. Almost every male wore a badge of some kind — of his school, institute, union or some special award — and perhaps such insignia went some little way to appease the people's hunger for some color in their lives. It would amuse me to notice that travelers getting into a plane, ship or train would look at badges before faces. But this was the first Master of Sport badge I had seen, and its owner turned out to be a master of motorcycle racing.

One cannot travel through the Soviet Union without realizing how whole-heartedly the Russians have taken to sports. The State may have organized them for reasons of prestige, but it could not have done so if the people themselves did not possess a natural love and aptitude for competitive exertions.

With our master motorcyclist at the wheel, we drove out of Irkutsk, past the high school where the poet had been educated. He pointed out a stand of poplars, light dripping like water from their trembling leaves. "Twenty-six of us left from this school on the same day for the war," he told me, "and before we left, we each planted a poplar. Only five of us came back."

Soon we came to the side of a hill overlooking the broad Angara River. It was smooth and silent there, thanks to the hydroelectric dam that had been built across the rapids. But before that, the poet said, it had been a wild, swift, passionate river. Swimming it, when he was a child, had been a hazardous business.

Now he spoke to me of Lake Baikal. It was the deepest fresh-water lake in the world — 5,700 feet deep. The water entering it by river, even a drop of rain, took four hundred years to make its way out and leave by the Angara. That was due not only to its depth and size but also to the hot springs in its bed, which sent warm water flowing up and thus drew the cold water down. Baikal was so big that if all its tributaries were sealed off, the water in it would still take four hundred years to empty.

Even more remarkable was the fish and animal life in and around the lake. There was a delicious kind of Baikal salmon, found nowhere else. There were also the Baikal seals, perhaps 40,000 of them, of which the Buriat hunters (the Mongols who inhabited this part of Siberia first) were allowed to kill about 3,000 every year for their fur. But imagine seals thousands of miles from the Arctic Ocean — marooned here, he believed, by the last Ice Age. Then there were the great mountain bears that came down to the lake in winter, going three or four miles out on the ice to fish in the holes made by the Buriats.

No river I have ever seen poured out of a great lake with such eagerness as did the Angara out of Baikal, and its flow held all our attention until the road rounded the head of the gorge and suddenly we saw the lake. Its waters were blue as a bowl of Bristol glass, and they vanished unimpeded across the horizon as if to join the Pacific Ocean. The fleets of ships which ply up and down the lake, from one Buriat village to another, were setting out on their first voyage after a winter in frozen harbors. They sailed on unruffled water that looked like an endless sea. In the distance I saw the tall Sayan Mountains of Mongolia and caught one remote flash of snow from the giant Mongdhu-Sardik.

We drove as far as the road would take us, which was only a mile or two because the main communications around the lake are by water. The official pensions and rest houses — rough, homely establishments — were just opening for the season. Hard by the shore we found a restaurant open and sat down to a delicious meal of black Siberian bread and butter, smoked Baikal trout and thick fried steaks of the incomparable Baikal salmon.

At the Master of Sport's suggestion the poet and I went home by river, through the sunset, in one of those enormous jet-propelled hydrofoils which are all the fashion in the Soviet Union. Back at Irkutsk, the electric lights were suddenly switched on. The effect by that wild river, in that rugged setting, was startling. I had not yet learned to associate the heart of Siberia with such prodigious power.

My guides insisted I look into the sources of that power, but the poet had no heart for it and excused himself. Next morning they took me out to the power station built into the walls of the dam across the Angara. The engineer in charge for the day, a woman in her thirties, showed us over the installation. There were many features about it that I could neither appreciate nor follow, but I learned that the dam was remarkable in not being built entirely of concrete. A gap was left between the concrete supports on either bank, and this was closed by the new method of dumping rocks and gravel into the powerful river.

The whole of Irkutsk turned out night and day to watch the dramatic and controversial operation. Long lines of trucks drove up without pause to tip great boulders into the stream, for the process had to be continuous to be successful. Hundreds of newspapermen and official observers from far and wide were there. On the last day the excitement was almost unbearable until suddenly, during the afternoon, a lorry tipped another load of boulders in the surging river and a head of stone showed steady above the surface. Thousands of spectators held their breath. Could the stone hold in such angry water? It held. Soon there was not only a broad wall of boulders across the gap but a working bridge as well, and the trucks could cross from one bank to the other. The eyes of the woman engineer shone as she described the feat. This, I gathered, was the damming method Russian engineers were using in the new Aswan Dam on the Nile. The Irkutsk project, she emphasized, was a real breakthrough in hydroelectric construction.

I had been so impressed by the Irkutsk hydroelectric scheme that I wanted to go on to Bratsk. I encountered the usual difficulties, but the poet announced quietly that he would arrange the matter in four or five days' time. Meanwhile, in between telephoning and disappearing to interview officials, he helped me to see his pleasant friendly, provincial city. Like all important Russian towns, he said, Irkutsk grew up at the crossing of many ancient routes — to China, Mongolia, Afghanistan, Alaska and Moscow. In his youth it was a city made almost entirely of wood. I could see for myself how it had changed — he nodded at the distant factory chimneys, the new apartment blocks and new houses on the west bank — yet a great deal of the old remained.

One day the Master of Sport drove me deep into the country to look at state and collective farms. On one farm I visited, the chairman told me it had three villages and 10,000 persons of all ages, and that it was still growing. Every year, he said, they cleared another 2,000 acres of *taiga* for cultivation. I regret to say I did not believe him. Being a farmer myself, I had some bitter experience in Africa with clearing bush and forest for cultivation, and I was certain he had neither the machinery nor the manpower to do so much in a year. When he told me that his farm made 50 per cent profit on the capital invested, I stopped making notes.

The self-deception about agriculture, at all levels, was as shameless as it was fashionable in Russia. Even here in Siberia the officials tried to deceive me — perhaps out of duty, patriotism or fear, all of which I could understand. They were small men caught up in a system and forced to make a machine work which was basically of the wrong design. There were few farmers in charge of farms. Party secretaries and factory foremen were the types one usually found in command. This Siberian chairman was a mechanic.

Now he told me that this huge farm was just being transformed from a collective into a state farm.

"How do your farmers feel about that?" I asked.

"They are all rejoicing," he said. "After all, now they run no risks and get a good salary whatever the harvest."

But I had never seen faces less joyful than those of the peasant workers hanging around the chairman's office. Besides, I had only to look at the individual plots allowed to each peasant to see where their love, imagination and care had gone. It was no good pretending that these people did not feel cheated. The Revolution had worked a confidence trick on them all. They had revolted in order to have the land to themselves. But no sooner was the Revolution consolidated than a far more inflexible landlord, the State, had taken it away from them again in the name of collectivization.

The moment came when the poet proved as good as his word and produced permission and tickets for me to fly to Bratsk with one guide. We took off just before sunrise on a cloudless morning, in what my companion called a "wild" plane. There was no hostess and we all helped ourselves to seats as best we could. I could find none with an unbroken safety belt. The cabin looked as if it had been neither swept nor dusted for weeks, and the air pressure was not controlled.

Our route took us by way of the new industrial towns of Angarsk, Cheremkhovo, Tulun and Taishet. Angarsk, though not the biggest city, was Siberia's pride. Only a few years ago it consisted of a handful of peasants who kept goats, consumptive cattle and a few scraggly horses and grew potatoes and cabbages. Today it has a population of around 200,000. An army officer in our plane proudly declared there was nothing in Angarsk that was not modern and new. Why, it had cafeterias just as in the United States!

We landed at Tulun for breakfast — one of the best I had in the Soviet Union. I ate the freshest of eggs and ham, bread hot from the oven and unsalted butter yellow as a marigold, and I drank milk with the cream thick on top. Then we headed due north and left the new world quickly behind. The cultivated clearings vanished utterly to leave us with nothing but brooks, streams, rivers and *taiga*. As mile after mile of this went by, it seemed less and less credible that we could be on the way to what the Russians say is the world's greatest hydroelectric project.

At Bratsk we were met by a schoolmaster in company with the editor of the hydroelectric workers' paper, *Angara Lights.* The two men proved delightful guides. They spoke with much laughter of the challenges faced by those who built the dam. One had been the midges — the Siberian midges of summer rising like smoke out of the *taiga,* stinging, beating the air away from people's faces so that they came near to being stifled. Moscow, true to form, had forgotten to supply the workers with nets, and work came to a standstill until they arrived.

There were also those first terrible winters which young workers from the metropolitan west had to endure, shivering in tents. A great many had to be sent home, but most of them remained until permanent quarters could be built. I could see for myself, the editor said, how successfully that had been done. He pointed to the outskirts of Bratsk, which we were just entering. I could scarcely believe my eyes. On that dry sunny day, with dust on the road and the great Siberian pine trees standing all around, I might have been entering a well-to-do suburb called Pinelands outside Cape Town in South Africa. Instead of the barrack blocks which still cluttered my memory, I looked on a world of individual houses, each of a different design and with a garden of its own.

"We call this part of Bratsk 'India,'" the editor said. "That is short for 'individual,' because it is given over entirely to people who want houses of their own design."

We stopped at an inn on the edge of India. It was built entirely of wood, the grain inside polished to shine like good leather, the windows covered by curtains of red, mauve and amber stripes. It was the gayest and most attractive hotel I saw in the whole of the Soviet Union. A large double bedroom with a kitchen and a bathroom was put at our disposal. Beside the bed was a table with a reading lamp and a telephone. I might have been in the best Swiss chalet.

"Wouldn't you like to telephone your home in London?" our host asked me. We were deep in the bush, some three hundred miles from Irkutsk, and Irkutsk was more than three thousand miles from Moscow. I looked so amazed that they all laughed and insisted. The call made, they hurried me out to the dam, where we spent the rest of the day.

I cannot, of course, pronounce on the giant installation technically. All I know is that everyone I met, from engineers to concrete mixers, despised all other kinds of projects and pitied all other workers. And I met a great many workers that day: the moment we stepped out on the wall of the dam, high above the waters of the river, I was told, "Look at our slave labor. Please stop and speak to anyone and ask any questions you like."

Some workers, perhaps, were instinctively keeping up national appearances in front of a foreigner. But most, I believe, were sincere. They felt a sense of superiority and satisfaction — of a downright snobbery that went with hydroelectric work. When Bratsk was finished, as it soon would be, giving out its 4,600,000 kilowatts of power, they expected to move 180 miles farther north and deeper into the *taiga*, where another hydroelectric site on the same river was already surveyed and waiting for workers like themselves.

Next day I left Irkutsk by train for Moscow in order to catch the plane that was to take me to the Far East. So as not to lose Siberian continuity, I flew back at once. The plane was the biggest in which I have ever traveled. On earth it looked so huge that one doubted its capacity to fly, and once in the sky it had a tail wobble like a whale and trembled all over.

We left Moscow soon after ten, flew for eight hours without a stop and landed at Khabarovsk at three the following morning. On the way I caught no sight of the great Siberian cities; only the essentials of land, river, forest and broken blue hills, untouched by man. Then, with melodramatic suddenness, the great chains of light of Khabarovsk appeared, smoking in the first monsoon rain, to tell the same story of expansion in Siberia. Early as it was in the morning, I counted ten planes as large as mine drawn up outside the airport building, which was itself crowded with people. The guide who met us told me every hotel and inn was full. He had with great difficulty got me a room in the main hotel. My Russian companion from Moscow, he regretted to say, would have to share a room with three others.

On my first morning in Khabarovsk, a city of more than 300,000 people, I stood amazed on the banks of the Amur River, the other epic stream of the Soviet Union. Up to now it had been little more than a mirage of history in my imagination, but here it was a great contemporary waterway swollen and still swelling with rain. Its surface was burdened with traffic— steamers, barges, fishing boats and above all tugs towing vast cigar-shaped rafts of lumber. Where the river met the horizon, bridges worthy of those of the Hudson and Mississippi carried the railway and road on south to Vladivostok.

Neither the Russians nor the Chinese, who share its upper reaches, have yet been able to control this massive stream in the season of the monsoon rains. It rises swiftly and relentlessly, and on one occasion it rose so high that a ship sailed down the main street of a town along its banks. Almost as big as the Amur are its tributaries, in particular the great Ussuri, which joins it near Khabarovsk. No wonder the people I met were full of plans for using this excess of water, which yearly flooded the low-lying and densely populated land in the Amur basin. One plan was to cut canals to link the Amur with the Tatar Strait as well as with the Sea of Japan near Vladivostok.

Later we drove on abominable roads deep into the forest, which stepped in at once to surround the city. So varied was the climate that the trees of north and south, of cold, hot and temperate zones, all grew here together — a world of botany gone mad. Even more mixed-up, my friends assured me, were the birds and animals that invested these sepulchral woods. There were, to mention only a few, the great Siberian tiger, the leopard, black and gray wolves and a unique species with bright red fur, the brown and black bear, an antelope with wool like sheep, tortoises without shells, elk, spotted deer, a tiny tree-fern deer hardly bigger than a rat. In the rivers lived ninety different kinds of fish.

In this forest the peasant clearings looked braver than most. There was an increasing number of these because one of the prides of Khabarovsk is its scheme to make itself self-sufficient in vegetables. It has an average of 256 cloudless days a year, and some pioneering spirit had the bright idea to use the sun for growing produce under glass. As a result, an empire of collective glass houses is beginning to advance along the valleys and probe deeper into the woods.

Everywhere the glass-house tycoons were grumbling over the damage that bureaucracy, overcentralization and bottlenecks were doing to their plans, but to me the scale of those plans was most impressive. I thought again how fundamentally Russia is a "marathon" country. It is not the short-distance sprints, the egg-and-spoon and three-legged races of life that catch the national imagination, but the impossible long-distance obstacle race and the victory against tremendous odds. They do not count the cost in time, money or human material. "If only we had more manpower," they would say ruefully to me. Before the war the population of this part of Siberia was not quite 3,000,000. Already it has risen to some 13,000,000, I was told — and even so the growth is not fast enough for Siberians.

Yet in this longing for manpower I thought I detected another factor. Only a few miles away lies China, as overcrowded and poor in natural resources as this land is empty and rich — and a shocking history of broken treaties and pledges lies like a shadow between Chinese and Russians. All this part of Siberia had once been a Chinese-Mongol sphere of influence. Can the Chinese continue to overlook the Russian penetration into this land of incalculable riches? Can they endure indefinitely having too little, with close at hand so few having too much? One doubted it, and I believe in their secret hearts the Siberians doubt it too.

The Westernness of Siberia had constantly struck and amazed me, but here in the Far East the people seemed to me more Western than ever and the least Asiatic and Oriental of any group I encountered on my travels in the Soviet Union. And this was, for me, the main lesson of my probe to the Far East.

The conclusion thrust itself on me one day. A Russian acquaintance had taken us for an excursion by motorboat on the Ussuri. We went up it until we could see where it crossed the Chinese frontier between two low blue hills. "The Chinese patrol boats," he said, "are just around the next far bend. I don't think we had better go any farther."

I stood up to have a closer look at the hills, and I heard pronounced behind me, in slow deliberate English: "Oh, East is East and West is West, and never the twain shall meet."

It came over me then, with a dazzle of illumination, that for him and for all the people I had met in Siberia, this was the West and China was the East.

In that setting and that context, it was not particularly strange that Kipling, the great poet of British imperialism, should speak for the contemporary Russian.

VI

Riga and Leningrad

The United States and Britain have never recognized the incorporation into the Soviet Union of the Baltic states of Lithuania, Latvia and Estonia during the last war. Yet these states are so bound into the Soviet system that it seemed unrealistic to me not to sample life in at least one of them. I chose Riga, the capital of Latvia, which was not far from my next major stop, Leningrad.

The act of incorporation looked complete and final in Riga, at least superficially. The streets have been renamed after Russian comrades whose appeal to the emotions of the Latvian people can hardly be great. The main street bore Lenin's name, and there was a Gorki Street and a Kirov Avenue. Moreover, I was aware of the presence of Russian soldiers in greater proportions than I had encountered on normal occasions elsewhere. There were a dozen or so senior staff officers at my hotel alone, and I saw the soldiery well represented in the streets and places of amusement. This may have had nothing to do with the fact that we were on what is, in effect, conquered territory, but it was so marked an aspect of the scene that I could not ignore it.

At first glance too the signs of the shaping of the local economy appeared to be on the Russian model. One of the great official success stories is the Riga Fishermen's Collective, and I think there is no doubt that its material success is very real. The fishermen's cottages and apartment houses, their theater and concert halls, schools, clinics and offices look incredibly prosperous. Every year more and more Latvian ocean-going trawlers feel their way out of the Baltic Sea and intrude into the fishing grounds of the West and even those of Newfoundland and the North American littoral. These ocean-going crews are the well-paid *élite* of the Fishermen's Collective. The apartments in which I interviewed some of their skippers are bigger and better furnished than those of many established writers and university professors that I saw in Moscow. And all this is just a beginning. The skippers and their colleagues in the neighboring states are determined to develop long-distance trawling in a much bigger way.

This and much else made the Soviet conquest of the Latvian spirit appear conclusive. Yet after a while one began to wonder. I would drive back from Riga Beach, or one of the new workers' districts, and look across the broad Dvina River at the city's lovely skyline. Riga is one of the older cities of Europe, founded some 800 years ago. The spires of its many churches, the yellow castle walls, the gabled houses, the Assembly Hall of the medieval guilds and orders of Baltic chivalry — all were there as tranquil and translucent as any of Vermeer's views of Delft. I just could not believe that all the history and meaning expressed in that view could have been abolished.

My doubts seemed confirmed by my chauffeur, who spontaneously took exception to the one postwar feature prominent on Riga's skyline — the university building, an edifice in the rigid Soviet model.

"It's wrong!" he exclaimed, without fear of my Russian interpreter and our official guide. "It doesn't fit our style of architecture and should never have been built. We'll not let it happen again."

Later, wandering around the narrow dark streets of the old city, I found dozens of ancient churches, still intact and functioning. I also heard a great many people practicing the piano. Riga's long tradition of culture and music was still living. In that sense, the city in which Wagner had once been a musical director, Clara Schumann received with honors, and Liszt given an enthusiastic reception, was still an outpost of the classical European spirit.

My Latvian excursion served well as an introduction to Leningrad. Without it, I might not have realized so clearly how European the city of Peter the Great is. Visually, of course, one could not have failed to recognize the supremely European expression of its architecture and design. But despite the Revolution and some decades of Soviet indoctrination, the city's mind, spirit, behavior and inborn values and affinities still seem to be of northern Europe.

This is all the more significant because, as cities go, Leningrad is young, dating no farther back than the early eighteenth century. It would hardly have had time to create so much of a mind and spirit of its own if this creation were not part of an ancient urge and indeed one of the great fundamentals of the Russian soul. And this is based on the instinctive determination of the Russian people, undismayed and undiminished throughout their hapless, tragic, random centuries, not to be separated from the rest of Europe.

Here in Leningrad I realized that this urge is by no means expended. And I felt this to be the most important impression of all the many I had gathered on my long journey. It is urgent for the Western world — and indeed for the Russians too — to realize that in their deeps they are a part of Europe. All this talk about Russians being half Asiatic and half European seemed to me valid only in externals. The Russians are basically a European people — though admittedly with an important difference which presently I shall try to define.

The glamour of the European invasions of Russia, led by such dramatic characters as Napoleon and Hitler, is out of proportion in the total perspective of Russian history. They have left deep scars, of course, but given their own context of time and place, they are like a series of frontier skirmishes. The real trauma of Russia's history, the one which came nearest to extinguishing the Russian will and from which the modern Russian spirit still suffers most, was caused by invasion from the east and southeast, and above all by the prolonged Tatar domination of the land. The history of the Tatar invasion itself I find difficult to read, even at this distance of time, because of its sustained and unmitigated horror. All in all I suspect that, bright and wary as is the eye that Russia keeps on Europe, it is casual and trusting in comparison with that long, constant, over-the-shoulder look toward the east.

The fashionable explanations for the many estrangements between Europe and Russia are well known. But what is not recognized, perhaps, is the deeper cause of this split, which grows out of a profound inner difference between them. And the difference, as I see it, is this: the Russians are to this day still a relatively primitive people. The true destructive contribution of the Tatars to Russian history is that they retarded the natural evolution of a primitive society by keeping it, for centuries, a society on the run. Thus the Russians are naturally a communal people because they are basically a primitive people: and primitive man is naturally collective.

This, however, did not spring to my mind immediately I arrived in Leningrad. After my long journey in the interior I was inclined to be suspicious of the city. It looked so completely, beautifully European that I thought it too good to be true. I was inclined to think it self-conscious and conceived as a cold act of statesmanship. Even the site of the city was unbelievably pitched in some of the worst marshland in the Russian northwest, as if deliberately to demonstrate disdain of cost and an expertise in the art of the impossible.

Something of all this undoubtedly is present in Leningrad, but of course there is a great deal more. As I walked around it daily, I became more aware that the architects of the city, foreigners as well as Russians, had caught the excitement of Peter's break-through into Europe. They conceived their works in a state of intoxication arising from the largeness of both occasion and place. Only one among them, a Scot named Cameron, kept his head and introduced buildings so obedient to classical proportion that among the others they look like a few lone Presbyterians determined to stay sober on New Year's Eve. The imaginations of the Italians, in particular, spilled over easily like waterfalls. Carlo Bartolomeo Rastrelli designed a Winter Palace of 2,000,000 square feet, with 1,050 rooms, 117 staircases, 1,786 doors and 1,945 windows. And all this was done on land cleared in dense marsh forest, the earth so soft that the buildings had to be laid on piles driven deeply down. The labor force was composed of serfs brought in from all over Russia and so poorly equipped that in the beginning they had to scrape and dig the earth with their bare hands. The violence of the urge and the passion behind the will that raised this city can only be measured by reckoning with the immense suffering that went into it.

The tsars and the aristocracy filled their palaces with furnishings and fashions increasingly lush. In the museums of the Hermitage — as the Winter Palace is now called — and of the Kremlin in Moscow, much of the frenzy, splendor, fantasy and disregard of reality in Russian history invest the objects flashing in their glass cases. Dazed and amazed, I looked at hundreds of damascene sword blades and gold stilettos, a cape spangled with 120,000 pearls, brocaded, enjeweled dresses that took two years to make, and dozens of crowns, orbs and scepters ablaze with emeralds, diamonds, topazes and garnets. There were bridles for horses, too, in which the leather was hidden by the gold and jewelry riveted onto them, and there were saddle blankets made out of thousands of peacock and parrot feathers. There were golden spoons and soup ladles, silver wine flagons some four feet high with necks adorned in gold and emeralds, and a single set of two thousand silver pieces presented by Catherine the Great to one of her lovers.

Fortunately, there was also a serious purpose to the foundation of Leningrad, despite the excess with which it was perpetrated. Science, philosophy, education and the arts and skills of Western Europe found an enduring home there.

An observatory was built and a distinguished school of astronomy founded which, indeed, prepared the Russian spirit for the race to the stars. The first technological Russians, shipbuilders, industrialists, makers of lenses and clocks, the first great writers and intellects, the first rebels against despotism and the first believers in the freedom of the human spirit and conscience appeared and were nourished there. At the time of the First World War, no corner of Russia needed the Red Revolution less than the City of Peter did, and it is significant that even after the fall of imperial power this proud and self-critical capital had no liking for Bolshevism.

With a local girl I went to the Cathedral of St. Nicholas; she herself went there twice a year, she explained, not for devotions but for the music and the singing. She said the music of Bach and Tchaikovsky, heard in the setting for which it was created, was far more moving than in any opera house or concert hall.

I had never been in a church like this, a two-story green and white baroque edifice hard by a tranquil canal. On the ground floor two quite different ceremonies were taking place. On the left, people were queuing up and jostling one another in a feverish way in order to get to the font to have their babies baptized. On the right, four old men were lying in open coffins amid masses of white lilies, and groups of their relations, mostly middle-aged and old, stood around weeping without attempt to hide their tears.

"I warned you," the young woman whispered to me, "that you'd find mostly old people here." She indicated the mourners.

"But all those babies!" I protested. "I saw a number of very young couples at the font."

"That's only because their parents force them to do it," she countered.

We climbed up the wide staircase to look at the main congregation. The floor was packed with people standing between the slender columns, and the air was brilliant with the light of hundreds of candles, the vivid colors of the embroidered satin of the priests' clothes, and the flashing of jeweled crosses. The service was being conducted as much by the congregation as by the priests, as if a choir of many voices had joined to render a single transcendent chorale of Bach. Never have I heard such singing. The difference between this and the bleak, iconoclastic Protestant services to which I had been taken as a child, even the Anglican and Roman Catholic services I have attended all over the world, was overwhelming. Outside, I said something of this to the girl but she shook her head vigorously. "I am an atheist," she insisted. "I cannot take part in such superstitions. But the music and the singing were wonderful."

At that moment a young man in teddy-boy uniform came running through the gates into the churchyard, carrying a baby in his arms. Behind him, out of breath and wobbling on high-heeled shoes, came the mother of his child. Neither of them looked over twenty-one, and their anxiety to be in time for the mass baptism could not have been more obvious.

"You could hardly call that couple old," I said.

This articulate girl was silent for a while as she stared after them. Then she shrugged and said, "Well, what do you expect of teddy-boys, anyway?"

VII

Moscow Again

Only when I had finished exploring Leningrad did I feel ready to return to Moscow, to round off my journey with an uninterrupted stay of a fortnight. How different the capital looked now! I wondered how I could ever have thought its citizens dowdy. The women now looked relatively gay in their bright summer dresses, and the men seemed almost brisk. "You should have seen the Muscovites as we first saw them seventeen years ago," the wife of a diplomat told me. "The improvement in taste and variety of fashion is incredible, and every day the people become more demanding."

I still held to my first impression of Moscow as a village and still thought it a parochial capital, perhaps because I continued to be dazzled by the vision of Peter's great city. But on my travels I had picked up something of the Russian identification with the nation's capital. There is no

Page 153 The Hermitage from across the Neva River; 154 Midnight view of Annunciation Cathedral during the summer white nights in Leningrad; 155 Kira Azarova sits in her room of the old actors home in Leningrad. She is surrounded by mementos of her theatrical family, all of them dead now, many victims of the war with the Germans; 156 Leningrad Beach on the Neva River; 157 Children play at one of the Hermitage entrances; 158 Maya Plisetskaya, the first ballerina of Russia, takes her bows after a performance of *Don Quixote* at the Bolshoi; 159 Manazer, the Establishment sculptor, sits at the feet of a giant Lenin; 160 A woman railway worker guards her crossing. She is responsible for the decoration of her hut; 161 A boy sits in the window of a Pre-Revolutionary home near Moscow; 162 Young pioneer camp; 163 First grade class in a factory-sponsored school in a Moscow suburb; 164-165 Ice skaters in Moscow's Gorki Park; 166 Night view of Moscow from the Lenin hills; 167 Red Square and St. Basil's Cathedral; 168 Soviet citizens pass under giant Lenin mural. This mural is put up outside the Agricultural Exhibition grounds in Moscow on appropriate holidays and occasions.

СЛАВА КПСС!

doubt that all the roads of Russian feeling lead to Moscow. It is a central point where all the nuances of Russian character can meet. For most Russians it may be unattainable, but they need to feel it is there, if only as a focal point for their misery.

It was in this deeper, instinctive sense of what a capital can mean that Moscow now impressed me, and this impression was stimulated and maintained by the hours I spent at the Kremlin. Used as I had become to being tossed about between the magnanimity and the pettiness of the Soviet system, I was now overwhelmed by the freedom with which I was allowed to wander alone, except for a guide, sometimes for a whole day, through the innermost buildings of this ancient fortress. The lights were turned on in the immense crystal chandeliers of the Imperial Palaces while the two of us went slowly through the State rooms, galleries and boudoirs, dazzled and enchanted, like men who had fallen through a pothole in the road of time to find themselves in some treasure house of history.

Outwardly, the Kremlin looks an incongruous pile of shapes, styles and colors, but inwardly it assumes a strange consistency, as if it were not architecture but rather some geological formation of history wherein the elements that have shaped Russian destiny are deposited, layer upon layer, with chronological precision. Even the Palace of Congresses of the Soviets, the most successful and impressive modern building in Moscow, standing behind the burning red brick ramparts and beneath the gold bubble domes, seemed curiously to belong to the golden rooms of the tsars. This effect was brought about by the absolute manner in which the shape of the building is determined by its function: a single hall in one building serving a vast number of Russians. Eight thousand people can be seated in comfort in the main theater. I sat there twice with just such audiences and the hall did not look crowded. The stairs, escalators, corridors and doors are so designed that one can move easily from the ground floor to the restaurants above. After refreshment, one can walk leisurely along broad promenades walled in with glass, and see, level with one's eyes, the spires of the churches, the ancient crosses, crescents, domes, five-pointed stars — and, indeed, the television aerials — all rippling in the limpid light of a summer evening like coral shapes in a great aquarium.

Perhaps the most impressive of all the buildings belonging to the Kremlin complex is the Cathedral of St. Basil, built in the sixteenth century by Ivan the Terrible. Some intuition suggests that here, in bricks and mortar, is a complete statement of all that was invisible and searching in the Russian spirit. I contemplated it daily as one might study some cipher for which the key was missing. My first reaction was to lose patience with the building and dismiss it as mad, reflecting that the imagination which decreed it was also mad.

The Cathedral of St. Basil has no obvious symmetry, and its spires, domes and doorways are all of different styles and shapes. All the varied influences that have ever impinged on Russian life are present: Greek, Roman, Byzantine, Arab, Tatar and Gothic architecture is piled upon and around it. Even a hint of Babylon, Assyria and Scythia intrudes among the walls. No two domes are alike in height, shape or decoration. One is covered with gold, blue and green bands of plaster curving upward to a single point, so that it looks like a top spinning against the sky. Another displays a mosaic of tiles in horizontal zigzags of white and red. A third bristles with colorful greenish painted stucco. A fourth combines something of the three others. Hard by them are Gothic spires and spits of different heights piled on varying pagan foundations. It all appears ill-fitted for coherent worship, but in the middle of this wheeling, reeling system stands one tall triumphant spire looking like a tower of medieval Europe and ending in a round Russian turret of gold pointing a single cross at the massive sky.

Gradually, as one becomes familiar with this church, it begins to make sense, acting within one's imagination like the impurity within the shell of an oyster around which a rare pearl grows. The building came to imply to me a profound and organic meaning. It conveyed to me something of the urgent necessity of making whole the many and varied fragments of the past, the boundless possibilities, conflicting trends, the paradoxes and tensions of this immense land and its people. In this church the past, present and the future, too, were there before me as in a symbol so vivid that it could awake the sleeper from his dreams. Indeed the man who built it had done for Russia what the architects of the Renaissance did for Europe. This is an original statement of a purely Russian renaissance, a reawakening that has already taken many bewildering, cruel and contradictory forms, and even so has hardly yet begun.

What is even more disquieting and archaic is that the State can and does at any moment take the dispensation of justice into its own hands and direct its course to suit a trend of policy. Thus one of the most distressing features of the cases of currency infringement which came up for trial while I was in Russia was the deliberate attempt to attach all blame on the Jews. The trouble is that systems which claim infallibility, as does the Soviet system, cannot do without scapegoats. Since it cannot itself be wrong, it can only be wronged. So, like a primitive despot, it is forever sending its witch doctors far and wide through the land to smell out persons on whom it can blame the national afflictions. I fear that, within the State, the Russian Jews are cast in the same sacrificial role that capitalist societies play in the world without.

However, there is a second world, apart from the Kremlin, around which Moscow life revolves, and that is the world of the new university in the Lenin Hills. In this center of intellect and technology, it is impressive to see how the Soviet system is being reappraised and challenged.

The new university building is the highest in the city, dominating the skyline from afar. The figures alone are impressive: over 17,000 students, nearly 2,000 laboratories, 1,500 rooms, 65 miles of corridors, 115 lifts, not to mention several cinemas, swimming pools, cafeterias and libraries full of Russian and foreign books. It is unfortunate that, away from the main staircases and behind the gilt, bronze, marble, granite, porphyry and alabaster, the old indifference to detail emerges and the woodwork is rough, the staircases and floors already worn. Yet even the briefest of contacts here with individual writers, artists and scientists is enough to suggest that the old system is becoming more flexible.

I was amazed to find how light was the impact of the Revolution on the values of the young. They are intensely patriotic, and they are proud of Russia's achievements with a passion that can be understood only against the backwardness which has haunted Russian lives for long, incoherent centuries. Even the present-day system, so rigid and unpalatable to me, has emerged for them as something far more representative of the people than anything they have ever enjoyed before. Yet I felt that the young were most fortunate in that their Revolution was truly over and they were free not only to be bored by it but to begin their own reformation. This, perhaps, is one of the reasons the old writers and artists feel so bitter about the new trends among the "ungrateful" young, and why the aging Party stalwarts stand at bay, like old bulls in danger of being driven from the herd they have protected from so many dangers.

In Russia the young accept fully the necessity for their Revolution — but that is all. More and more they seem anxious to get away from it, as if it had been some terrible interruption of their natural evolution, which they want to take up again where it left off. I thought I saw in them a reawakening of an instinctive sense of kinship, by right of birth, with the great complex of the European spirit. Politically the new Russian is a loyal person who will surrender conscience and heart to the State. But in matters of taste, mind and personal feeling, increasingly he tries to follow his European inclination. Already he finds it quite natural to stress the importance of an artist, scientist or writer by saying, "His work is known in the West". Most significant of all, he is beginning to believe it his patriotic duty not only to refuse to follow blindly the political lead in matters of art and taste but even to criticize and resist it.

Similarly the scientist and the technologist, whose success and efficiency depend on a regard for objective truth, find it hard to subordinate their work to Marxist-Leninist doctrine — as they had to do under Stalin in the infamous episode in which Lysenko affirmed the inheritance of acquired characteristics. The politician may still strive to reconcile scientific truth with his Leninist revelation, just as Victorian England made scientific validity subject to Old Testament standards and thus rejected Darwin's theory of the origin of species. But the contemporary Russian scientist clearly has no interest in such adjustments. His taste for the whole truth, long denied satisfaction at the front door of the system, has now found nourishment and is growing lusty on scraps fed to it at many a rear entrance.

The changes are immense in industry and commerce, too. In these areas the shedding of ideological shackles has already gathered a resounding momentum which everywhere brings its influence to bear, even in the small foreign community in Moscow.

Then there is the new intellectual world of painters, writers and artists. Whatever the State and Party may demand of them, they have their own ideas of their duty to their art.

Among these young, the interest in the pure form, patterns and images communicated directly from life itself is as great as if they, too, wanted to start with their own vision. For the first time in the history of Russian painting it is significant that some of the most gifted painters concentrate on self-portraiture, as if in recognition of the supreme need in Russian man to discover his individual self, which has been so neglected in the primitive practice of collective values.

I felt this all the more keenly as I watched the pressures of the State forcing artists, writers and poets to recant their living faith, as even Yevtushenko was forced to do, and I felt certain they were being driven to recant by a belief that it was patriotically necessary, and because the umbilical cord between their newly born individual modern selves and this ancient, primitive Mother Russia has not yet been cut.

I thought of Boris Pasternak, who was the first to break through the barrier between Russia and the outside world by publishing his *Dr. Zhivago* abroad. I am ashamed to say that in my own world, where we still take communication of this kind for granted, I did not fully appreciate the greatness of his achievement. I had to go to Russia and experience the power of the State and the Establishment, the immense primitive insistence on like-mindedness as the greatest of all values, to appreciate what he had done. To the new Russian writers he is the first Soviet literary saint and martyr, and I believe that because of him Russia will never be the same again.

It was significant to me how much he is discussed and what emotions he still arouses. The severest criticism I heard came from members of the Party and amounted in the main to the charge that he had been unpatriotic in publishing his book abroad. Only one, an unpleasant young Komsomolsk leader, said, "What do you expect of a Jew!" But even at these political, nonliterary levels, I was amazed by the numbers who said to me, "If it had happened now, I am certain *Dr. Zhivago* would not have been suppressed."

I went with a friend one weekend to the place where Pasternak is buried at Peredelkino. We had no difficulty in finding the spot, for we met a woman who seemed to know without asking why we had come and said, "You'll find his grave over there." The grave was apart, under some tall pines, carefully tended and covered with fresh flowers. It was what had been so strangely rare on my journey — an individual grave of a man individually mourned and remembered. It seemed to me that Pasternak, in his separateness, belonged more to the country he loved so deeply than did all those others in their collectivity of life and death.

The day before I left Russia, the Soviet authorities decided to bury someone in the Kremlin wall. They threw a police cordon all around my hotel and the squares nearby. I could not get through to say good-by to my friends at the British Embassy, to one of whom I owed fifty rubles. At the airport I asked the young Russian with me if he would be good enough to return the money for me, along with a note. He blushed with humiliation at a system which forced him to refuse a friend so obvious and easy a service, but he said firmly, "I am afraid that is quite out of the question."

And that, too, I thought, as I sat down in my seat in the British Comet, was Russia. I fastened my safety belt and looked up to see the English crew calmly going about their work. I thought I had never seen happier and more resolved expressions. Like the once ordinary girl in the poem, they were now full of mystery for me, the mystery of a freedom as yet unknown in Russia. Suddenly I felt so much lighter that I was almost giddy, as with lack of ballast. Until that moment I had not known what a weight in my spirit had been the Soviet system.